Profiles

A Collection
of Short Biographies

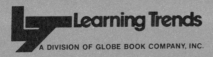 **Learning Trends**

A DIVISION OF GLOBE BOOK COMPANY, INC.

NEW YORK • CHICAGO • DALLAS

Profiles

A Collection of Short Biographies

Zacharie J. Clements

Leon F. Burrell

M. Jerry Weiss
Reading Consultant

ISBN: 0-87065-917-0

Copyright © 1975, Learning Trends,
a division of Globe Book Company, Inc.
175 Fifth Avenue, New York, New York 10010
Published simultaneously in Canada.

Consulting Editor: Mindy Rosenthal

Printed in the United States of America 1 2 3 4 5 6 7 8 9

AUTHORS

Zacharie J. Clements is Associate Professor of Reading Education at the University of Vermont. He has taught in public schools from grade 6 through high school. Dr. Clements has developed and implemented training programs in the teaching of corrective reading and reading in secondary-school content areas. He has conducted numerous teacher training institutes for the local, state, and national governments and has served as a consultant and lecturer to school districts throughout the United States and Canada. In addition, Dr. Clements is co-author of the Learning Trends Series, *World of Vocabulary.*

Leon F. Burrell is Assistant Professor in the College of Education and Social Services at the University of Vermont. Dr. Burrell previously served as a special education teacher and as a counselor in the Lansing (Mich.) public schools. He has been a major participant in human relations workshops and presentations throughout the country. Dr. Burrell is co-author of several books in the field of education and has contributed articles to several educational journals.

Reading Consultant

M. Jerry Weiss is Distinguished Service Professor of Communications at Jersey City State College. He is an experienced teacher of English, language arts, and reading at the secondary-school and college levels.

Dr. Weiss is the author of a number of language arts textbooks and professional books for teachers. He is on the Publications Board of the College Reading Association and is Chairman of the Publications Board of the New Jersey Council of Teachers of English.

Contents

Contents

To the student

We hope that you like this book. We have tried to make it interesting and easy to read. It is a collection of biographies, or stories about people. The people in it are real people. They have all helped to make America great. Their stories are true stories. We hope that by reading them you will get a better understanding of all Americans.

If you have trouble with any of the questions at the end of the stories, there is help for you—right in the book. At the back, there is a section called *Reading First Aid.* It has "cures" for the problems you might face as you answer the reading questions. There are explanations and sample exercises to help you become a better reader.

As you read this book, you will learn many new things about interesting people. Maybe one of them will remind you of someone you know—maybe even yourself!

Story 1

SEÑOR TENNIS

Everyone laughed at his fifty-cent racket.
Nobody laughed at his 112 m.p.h. serve!

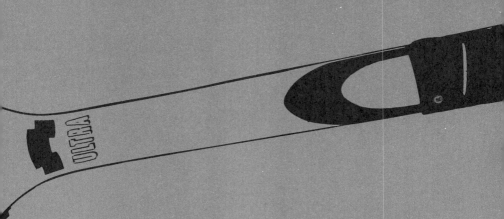

"Look at Pancho's funny racket. What a
cheap thing." All the boys laughed. *Richard
"Pancho" Gonzales* (gun ZAH lus) walked away
slowly. His mother was a poor Mexican-American.
She had bought him the racket for fifty cents.
It was all she could afford to give him for
Christmas. "I'll show them," thought Pancho.

For the next two years, he played tennis
day and night. He never seemed to tire. He
would watch good players for hours. Then he
would go off by himself and practice what they did.

3

By the age of 15, Pancho was the best young player in Southern California. Coaches were amazed. How could this boy do so well without any professional coaching? He had learned all his skills by himself!

Pancho was almost ready to try to become the United States champion. But in 1945, he was called to serve his country. He joined the Navy but continued to play tennis.

Shortly after leaving the Navy, Pancho started to become a national hero in tennis. In

1948 at the age of twenty, he won the United States Championship. The next year he won the championship again. He also played on the championship Davis Cup team that beat Australia.

Now Pancho was famous. His tennis serve was clocked at over 112 miles per hour. You could hardly see the ball. Pancho decided to become a professional. He would play for money.

He was the world's professional champion six times in a row. No one has matched this record. He was such a great player that many people came to see him. He never disappointed them. For over twenty years, Pancho Gonzales dominated tennis.

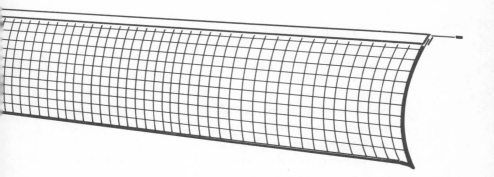

Pancho Gonzales was a poor Mexican-American. He started out with a fifty-cent racket and never had lessons. Yet he was proud and he was determined to succeed. Because of this, he became the greatest player in the world. He truly deserves the title "Señor Tennis."

Remembering

1. Which one of the following best states the *main idea* of paragraph 2? (Reread the paragraph.)
   a. Pancho often watched good players.
   b. Pancho never seemed to tire.
   c. Pancho practiced many hours to become a champion.
   d. Pancho practiced by himself.

2. Which one or more of the following are *facts* presented in the story?
   a. Pancho lived in Southern California.
   b. Pancho served in the U.S. Army.
   c. Pancho learned tennis from his high school coach.
   d. Pancho never became a professional.

3. Which one or more of the following are *facts* presented in the story?
   a. Pancho started with a $50.00 racket.
   b. Pancho won the world championship four times.
   c. Pancho played on the Davis Cup team.
   d. Pancho only played tennis for ten years.

4. Even though *it doesn't say so* in the story, you can tell that:
   a. Most championship players receive lessons.
   b. Pancho's mother was a good tennis player.

    c. The Davis Cup team almost lost to Australia.

    d. Pancho's serve was not very good.

5. Which of the following was mentioned *first* in the story?
   a. Pancho Gonzales won the Southern California Championship.
   b. Pancho was given a racket for Christmas.
   c. Pancho played on the Davis Cup team.
   d. Pancho served in the Navy.

6. The word *professional* (paragraph 6) means:
   a. playing for the fun of it.
   b. playing for money.
   c. playing in tournaments.
   d. changing the rules of the games.

7. The word *dominated* (paragraph 7) means:
   a. gave something.
   b. trained someone.
   c. controlled something.
   d. discussed something.

8. A *poor* title for this story would be:
   a. A Championship Tennis Player.
   b. Why It Pays to Try Hard.
   c. The Mexican-American Hero.
   d. The "Lucky" Tennis Player.

Discovering

Fun with Words: Scramble

Below are some of the words from the story. They are scrambled, or all mixed up. See if you can figure out what each word is. Write the words in your notebook. You can look back at the story for clues. Try your hardest!

1. cchngoai (para. 3)
2. pshpmchiiona (para. 5)
3. sfmaou (para. 6)
4. dmtchae (para. 7)

Find Out More

1. It is an honor for a country to win the Davis Cup Tennis Championship. Which countries won it for the years 1952, 1953, 1963, 1967, and 1972? Try looking in an almanac or an encyclopedia.

2. Tennis has many funny words used in it. Here are some. Can you find out what they mean?
   a. *love*
   b. *deuce*
   c. *ad*
   d. *set*
   e. *let ball*

No Laughing Matter

People first laughed at Morgan's invention.
But when it came time to save lives, nobody laughed.

Andrew Kelly knew he did not have long to live. He was trapped in the collapsed tunnel under Lake Erie. He did not know how long he had been there. The explosion that wrecked the tunnel had shattered his leg. Now deadly

gas and smoke were beginning to seep into the dark chamber. He was sure there was no hope for him and the other trapped miners.

There would have been no hope for the trapped men except for a black inventor named *Garrett A. Morgan.* Morgan had been working on his new invention, the gas mask. Most people laughed at the funny-looking "toy." They said it wouldn't work. But Morgan continued to work on his invention. He knew it *could* work.

News of the tunnel collapse reached Morgan while he was in nearby Cleveland, Ohio. He decided to use the gas mask to try to save the trapped miners. He would be risking his life. The gas mask was not fully tested.

Morgan, his brother, and some black friends rushed to the scene of the tunnel disaster and prepared to enter. Morgan warned his friends about the untested masks. In the tunnel, their lives would be in great danger. No one backed out of the dangerous mission. Wearing the new gas masks, the men entered the tunnel. Every miner was rescued, including Andrew Kelley, who was unconscious and near death.

Later that year, 1916, Garrett A. Morgan was awarded a gold medal of the City of Cleveland. He had shown great bravery in saving all the miners' lives. No longer were this great black inventor and his "funny" mask cause for laughter.

Remembering

1. Which one of the following best states the *main idea* of paragraph 1? (Reread the paragraph.)
   a. Andrew Kelley was a miner.
   b. Smoke and gas were in the tunnel.
   c. The miners were afraid.
   d. There was an explosion in a tunnel.

2. Which one or more of the following are *facts* presented in the story?
   a. The tunnel collapsed in 1926.
   b. Several rescuers refused to enter the tunnel.
   c. Garrett received the City of Chicago's gold medal for bravery.
   d. Garrett's mask was not fully tested.

3. Which one or more of the following are *facts* presented in the story?
   a. Garrett Morgan was an inventor.
   b. Several miners were killed.
   c. The tunnel was under Lake Michigan.
   d. People laughed at the gas mask.

4. Even though *it doesn't say so* in the story, you can tell that:
   a. All inventors are laughed at.
   b. The men who rescued the trapped miners were brave.

12

   c. Morgan went to the tunnel because Andrew Kelley was his friend.

   d. Morgan was the first man to receive the Cleveland City award.

5. Which one of the following was mentioned *first* in the story?
   a. Morgan won a gold medal.
   b. People laughed at Morgan's invention.
   c. There was an explosion in the tunnel.
   d. Morgan was working on the gas mask.

6. The word *disaster* (paragraph 4) means:
   a. something that causes loss of life or property.
   b. something that shows strength.
   c. a serious crime.
   d. an unusual discovery.

7. The word *unconscious* (paragraph 4) means:
   a. awake.
   b. dead.
   c. sick.
   d. not awake.

8. A *poor* title for this story would be:
   a. The Great Chicago Tunnel Disaster.
   b. A Black Inventor.
   c. An Invention That Saved Lives.
   d. The Black Gold Medal Winner.

Discovering

Fun with Words: Crossword Puzzle

Copy the crossword puzzle into your notebook. Then fill in the white boxes with the correct words.

If you do not know how to do crossword puzzles, check with your teacher or someone in the class who knows how to do them. They are fun to do. Try this one and you'll see what we mean.

Across
1. to fall in (para. 1)
4. put into action (para. 3)
5. not a liquid; air (para. 1)
7. name of a lake (para. 1)

Down
1. a place like a room (para. 1)
2. sounds of humor (para. 5)
3. all (para. 4)
6. to leak slowly (para. 1)

14

Discovering

Find Out More

1. The gas mask has helped save many lives. Do you know how a gas mask works? How could you find out? If you don't know, ask your teacher. Then see if you can find out the following things:
    a. What is there in the gas mask that cleans the air?
    b. How are gas masks used today?
    c. Were gas masks ever used in wars?

2. Sometimes pictures help people to understand things. Try to draw a picture of the gas mask showing each part and how it works.

15

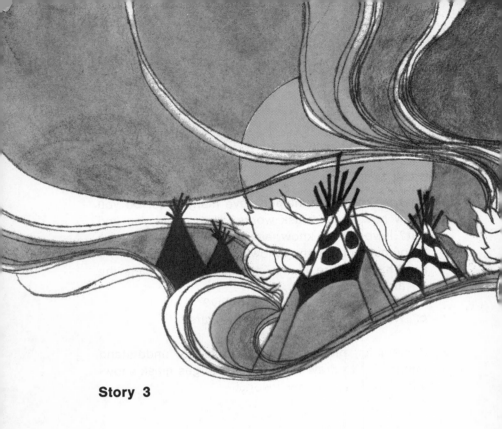

Medicine Man

*Could one Indian help save his people
from dying out? This one did!*

The four-year-old Apache boy awoke
screaming with fright. Shots were going off, and he
could see fires all about him. His mother and

father were nowhere around. Suddenly, the teepee caught fire and he crawled into the night. A wild scream made him shake with fear. He was snatched up by a warrior's arm and carried away into the night. Behind, the entire Apache village lay in ruins. The Pima tribe had made a successful raid.

The Pimas sold the boy to a Mexican-American reporter named Carlos Gentile (jen TEE leh). The reporter came to love the boy as a son, and he adopted him. He gave him the name *Carlos Montezuma* (mahn tuh ZOO muh).

Mr. Gentile took the boy with him on his travels around the country. With his quick mind, the young Apache quickly learned about reporting.

In 1881 when he was only 14, Carlos entered the University of Illinois. His own experience and all that he read convinced him that American Indians were being unfairly treated. He wished he could help his people. When he graduated, he entered medical school. As a doctor, he could be of great service to his people.

He became one of the first Indian doctors to enter the American Indian Service. He was angry and sad when he saw the Indians' land taken away and his people placed on reservations. These reservations were wastelands. There was little farming or hunting. His people were starving, sick, and uneducated. The once proud Indians were in danger of dying out.

Dr. Montezuma started hospitals to care for the sick. He founded schools and helped Indians get a decent education. He also taught his people about the world. He believed that the Indians could only improve themselves by leaving the reservation. They had to become part of the white man's world. He spent his whole life working for this dream.

Remembering

1. Which one of the following best states the *main idea* of paragraph 6? (Reread the paragraph.)
   a. Dr. Montezuma did much for his people.
   b. Dr. Montezuma wanted people to leave the reservation.
   c. Dr. Montezuma believed in education.
   d. Dr. Montezuma started hospitals.

2. Which one or more of the following are *facts* presented in the story?
   a. The four-year-old Indian was captured by the Apaches.
   b. Carlos entered college at age 14.
   c. Dr. Montezuma founded hospitals and schools.
   d. Carlos wanted to be a photographer for the newspaper.

3. Which one or more of the following are *facts* presented in the story?
   a. Carlos was sold to a reporter.
   b. Dr. Montezuma thought the reservations were good for Indians.
   c. The Pimas and Apaches were friends.
   d. Carlos hated reading.

4. Even though *it doesn't say so* in the story, you can tell that:
   a. Indian tribes were not always friendly to each other.

b. Carlos did not get along with his father.

c. Dr. Montezuma hated white men.

d. Indian reservations were usually good hunting lands.

5. Which of the following was mentioned *first* in the story?

    a. Carlos traveled with Gentile.

    b. Carlos entered the University of Illinois.

    c. The reservations were being improved.

    d. Carlos entered medical school.

6. The word *reservation* (paragraph 5) means:

    a. preventing something.

    b. a place to live.

    c. being certain.

    d. a ticket.

7. The word *wastelands* (paragraph 5) means:

    a. small pieces of land.

    b. deserts.

    c. places where a lot of people live.

    d. places not fit for human life.

8. A *poor* title for this story would be:

    a. An Early Indian Doctor.   **c.** A Famous Indian.

    b. The Indian Helper.   **d.** The Indian Wars.

Discovering

Fun with Words: Be a Word Detective

See if you can find the word that best fits each of the following. Try timing yourself to see how quickly (but carefully) you can get all the answers.

1. Which word means "a kind of house"? (para. 1)
2. Which word means "picked up quickly"? (para. 1)
3. Which word means "a kind of attack"? (para. 1)
4. Which word means "took as your own"? (para. 2)
5. Which word means "made you sure about something"? (para. 4)
6. Which word means "started something"? (para. 6)
7. Which word means "good; worthwhile"? (para. 6)

Discovering

Find Out More

1. The Pima and Apache Indians were mentioned in the story. Can you find out in which state they lived? Where are their reservations now? What is life like on their reservations?

2. Get together with your classmates to organize an "Indian Appreciation Day." You can make displays of different Indian tribes and their cultures. Go to your library, an American history book, or an encyclopedia to learn more about their life styles and people.

Sugar Daddy

Today sugar is plentiful, but once it was hard to get. Only the rich could afford it!

Sugar was like gold! Everyone loved the taste. But only the rich were able to afford it. Sugar was obtained from sugar cane and sugar beets. The process of removing the sugar was long and expensive. So the cost of sugar was very high. No one was clever enough to find a quick, cheap way to get it. Then a black man named *Norbert Rillieux* (REEL YUR) came along.

Norbert was born into slavery in Louisiana in 1806. His mother was a slave. His father was the white owner of the plantation where Norbert's mother lived and worked. As Norbert grew up, his father could see that his young son had great talent. He sent him to France to be educated. Norbert began to experiment with the sugar refining process.

He returned to Louisiana, educated and filled with ideas. Norbert was recognized as one of the most intelligent and creative men in the state. Soon he was ready to introduce his new sugar refining process. But he was black. Louisiana was a center of slavery and slave trading. Norbert was not allowed to participate in government, and he was bothered by police and white racists. When Norbert was told all free blacks must carry a pass in order to move about, he knew it was time to leave his homeland.

He returned to France. After ten years of hard work and struggle, his new sugar refining process was adopted. It was more successful than anyone had imagined. The cost of sugar production was cut in half. Sugar became available to everyone. In recognition of his work, the French government awarded Rillieux the highest award given in France, the Legion Pour Merité (POOR meh ree TAY). This great man could not live freely in his own country. He had to go to France to be recognized.

Next time you put sugar on cereal, buy candy, or enjoy anything sweet, you may remember that Norbert Rillieux made it possible. He was a real "Sugar Daddy."

Remembering

1. Which one of the following best states the *main idea of* paragraph 1? (Reread the paragraph.)
   a. Sugar came from beets.
   b. Norbert Rillieux came along.
   c. Sugar was very expensive.
   d. Everyone liked sugar.

2. Which one or more of the following are *facts* presented in the story?
   a. Rillieux was born in Louisiana.
   b. Rillieux was educated in Boston.
   c. Free blacks were required to carry a pass.
   d. Rillieux won the Legion Pour Merité.

3. Which one or more of the following are *facts* presented in the story?
   a. Rillieux's mother was a slave.
   b. Rillieux had a white father.
   c. Rillieux's father recognized his talent.
   d. Rillieux lived in France for a time.

4. Even though *it doesn't say so* in the story, you can tell that:
   a. In 1820, children of slaves could not be well educated in the United States.
   b. Rillieux's inventions were immediately accepted.
   c. Rillieux did not like France.
   d. After Rillieux's invention, sugar was hard to get.

27

Remembering

5. Which one of the following was mentioned *first* in the story?
   - **a.** Rillieux traveled to France for his education.
   - **b.** Rillieux was required to carry a pass.
   - **c.** Rillieux's invention was accepted.
   - **d.** Rillieux's father recognized his ability.

6. The word *plantation* (paragraph 2) means:
   - **a.** a large farm.
   - **b.** a kind of tree.
   - **c.** a home for Indians.
   - **d.** a kind of store.

7. The word *struggle* (paragraph 4) means:
   - **a.** a discovery.
   - **b.** effort and difficulty.
   - **c.** to hide.
   - **d.** to disappear.

8. A *poor* title for this story would be:
   - **a.** A Black Scientist.
   - **b.** Making Sugar Available for All.
   - **c.** A Black Man Who Had to Study in England.
   - **d.** How Sugar Refinement Was Discovered.

Discovering

Fun with Words: Synonyms

Words often have many meanings. Words that mean the same thing, or almost the same thing, are called *synonyms.* Below are several words that mean the same thing as a word used in the story. Look at the words and see if you can find the word in the story that has the same meaning.

1. method, procedure, plan, practice, routine: (para. 1)
2. facility, skill, capability, knack: (para. 2)
3. costly, dear, valuable, high-priced: (para. 1)
4. accepted, picked, chosen, selected: (para. 4)

Find Out More

The sugar on our tables comes from sugar beets and sugar cane. Try to find out how we get sugar from sugar cane and beets. See if Norbert Rillieux is mentioned when you read about sugar making. Some places to look are in an encyclopedia, in science books, and in the library catalog under "sugar."

THAT

LADY FROM RIO

She was a star in South America.
She became a star in North America.
She was truly an "all-American star."

Little María loved to sing and dance. She
dreamed of being an entertainer. This made her
father angry. He was a wealthy Brazilian merchant.
In South America, girls from good homes did
not dance on the stage. But María continued her
music lessons.

She was only fifteen when she began singing
on the radio. People in Rio de Janeiro, Brazil,
loved her style of singing. She decided she needed
a stage name. Her real name was María do Carmo
da Cunha (do KAHR mo dah KOO nyuh). This
was too long for anyone to remember. María
became *Carmen Miranda*.

In 1931, Carmen was only nineteen and already a star. Everyone in South America knew her name. Everyone wanted her records. Her music combined African and Indian beats. It had great rhythm and drive. She recorded over 300 records during the next few years. They were all best sellers. Her movies also became smash hits.

Carmen dreamed of coming to America. She tried to learn English. But when she spoke, she sounded funny. People enjoyed hearing her speak. Many people thought a South American

star would not make it in North America. But Carmen wanted to go.

In 1939, she got her chance. She came to America. Almost immediately, she became a star here. People loved to see her dance. They laughed at her jokes. They loved her singing. Her costumes were always colorful. Her hats became her trademark. They looked like fruit bowls filled with fruit. The "Carmen Miranda look" became very popular.

She went to Hollywood to make movies. She appeared in many films including *That Night in Rio, Down Argentina Way,* and *Weekend in Havana.* Millions of Americans saw her movies and loved her.

Carmen Miranda was now an international star. Her talent and charm touched all Americans. She helped people appreciate the talent of South Americans. She was the pride of all Spanish-speaking people. When she returned to Brazil, she was more popular than ever. In fact the President made that day a national holiday. This honor was well deserved.

Remembering

1. Which one of the following best states the *main idea* of paragraph 7? (Reread the paragraph.)
   a. Carmen had charm and talent.
   b. Carmen was an international star.
   c. Americans loved Carmen.
   d. Spanish-speaking people took pride in Carmen.

2. Which one or more of the following are *facts* presented in the story?
   a. Carmen's father wanted her to be a dancer.
   b. Carmen disliked dancing when she was young.
   c. Carmen performed in many movies.
   d. Few people bought Carmen's records.

3. Which one or more of the following are *facts* presented in the story?
   a. Camen lived in Argentina.
   b. Carmen wore colorful clothes.
   c. Carmen's music had a strong beat.
   d. Carmen spoke English well.

4. Even though *it doesn't say so* in the story, you can tell that:
   a. Carmen was never very popular.
   b. Brazilians were ashamed when Carmen tried to speak English.
   c. Stage names are usually short.
   d. Carmen left Hollywood because she did not like to make movies.

Remembering

5. Which one of the following was mentioned *first* in the story?
   a. Carmen wanted to come to North America.
   b. Carmen sang on the radio in Rio de Janeiro.
   c. The "Carmen Miranda look" became popular.
   d. A national holiday was made in Carmen's honor.

6. The word *trademark* (paragraph 5) means:
   a. a name.
   b. a kind of title.
   c. a way people or things are recognized.
   d. a discovery.

7. The word *wealthy* (paragraph 1) means:
   a. old.
   b. rich.
   c. well educated.
   d. talented.

8. A *poor* title for this story would be:
   a. The Brazilian Star.
   b. A Talented Painter.
   c. A Woman of International Fame.
   d. The South American Movie Star.

Discovering

Fun with Words: Match Antonyms

See if you can match the words in Column A to their *antonyms,* or opposites, in Column B. Look back in the story if you need to. Write the words in your notebook.

Column A

1. angry (para. 1)
2. colorful (para. 5)
3. hits (para. 3)
4. wealthy (para. 1)
5. popular (para. 5)

Column B

a. failures
b. poor
c. simple; dull
d. happy
e. brave
f. not liked

Find Out More

1. See if you can find any pictures of Carmen Miranda. Is she wearing one of her colorful hats? Try to draw one of these hats. Show it to your teacher and classmates.

2. Carmen Miranda's records are hard to find. See if you can locate one. Ask your parents, teacher, and librarian to help. What do you think of her music?

Vocabulary Review

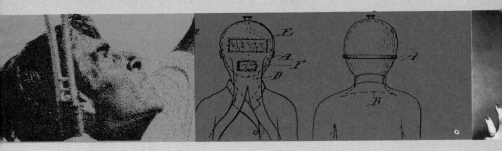

STORIES 1-5

Following are some of the words you learned in the stories you have read. See if you can remember what these words mean. Try your hardest. Write your answers in your notebook.

1. *Professional* means:
   a) playing for money.   b) a man who changes the rules.   c) playing in tournaments.   d) playing for the fun of it.

2. *Dominated* means:
   a) discussed.   b) trained.   c) gave.   d) controlled.

3. *Disaster* means:
   a) a joke.   b) a serious crime.   c) something that causes loss of life or property.   d) an unusual discovery.

4. *Unconscious* means:
   a) not awake.   b) awake.   c) sick.   d) unhappy.

5. *Reservation* means:
   a) a ticket. **b)** being certain. **c)** a place to live.
   d) preventing something.

6. *Wastelands* means:
   a) small pieces of land. **b)** places where a lot of
   people live. **c)** deserts. **d)** places not fit for people to live.

7. *Struggle* means:
   a) a discovery. **b)** a place to hide. **c)** to disappear. **d)** effort and difficulty.

8. *Plantation* means:
   a) a kind of store. **b)** a home for Indians. **c)** a
   large farm. **d)** a green plant.

9. *Trademark* means:
   a) a name. **b)** a kind of title. **c)** the way people
   or things are recognized. **d)** a discovery.

10. *Wealthy* means:
   a) old. **b)** rich. **c)** well educated. **d)** talented.

Story 6

Hideyo

Noguchi, M.D.

This man saved millions of American lives.
But he could not become an American citizen!

You hear the snake's warning rattle. You
freeze with fear. You can't see him. Suddenly,
the rattlesnake strikes. You feel his fangs enter
your leg. You stumble away. Your leg is on
fire with pain. You know death is near. Can
you reach your camp in time? Will you get help?

Thanks to a Japanese-American named
Dr. *Hideyo Noguchi* (hee DEH yo no GOO chee),
you would probably not die. The snakebite serum
he discovered has saved many thousands
of lives. Here is his story.

Hideyo lived in Japan with his parents,
who were very poor. One day his hand was
badly burned in a fire. Because his parents were
poor, he received no medical aid. As a result,
his hand was crippled. Because of this injury
and his family's poverty, Hideyo faced a hopeless
life. But his teacher realized that the boy

had great ability. The teacher arranged for an operation and for Hideyo's schooling. Hideyo decided on a career in medicine because he wanted to help other people as he had been helped.

After Hideyo became a doctor, he traveled all over the world studying terrible diseases like yellow fever and snake poisoning. He came to America to study and try to develop cures for these diseases. After being in America for several years, he wanted to become a citizen of the United States. But he was unable to. He was Japanese. There were laws to prevent Japanese and Chinese from becoming citizens. They were allowed to work and live here. They could not become citizens.

He was hurt and disappointed, but he continued to help Americans. Dr. Noguchi loved his "adopted country."

Yellow fever was killing thousands of people in South America. Dr. Noguchi decided to try to find a cure. While working day and night, he caught yellow fever and died before finding a key to the disease.

Though he died trying to help mankind, his one wish never came true. He never was granted *official* citizenship in America. But this great Japanese-American is a man all Americans can be proud of.

Remembering

1. Which one of the following best states the *main idea* of paragraph 3? (Reread the paragraph.)
   a. Hideyo had a hard life.
   b. Hideyo burned his hand.
   c. Hideyo's parents were poor.
   d. Hideyo needed an operation.

2. Which one or more of the following are *facts* presented in the story?
   a. Dr. Noguchi's parents were poor.
   b. Young Hideyo injured his leg.
   c. Dr. Noguchi died in South Africa.
   d. Dr. Noguchi wanted to become an American citizen.

3. Which one or more of the following are *facts* presented in the story?
   a. A teacher helped Hideyo.
   b. Chinese people could become American citizens.
   c. Dr. Noguchi studied in England.
   d. Dr. Noguchi discovered a cure for yellow fever.

4. Even though *it doesn't say so* in the story, you can tell that:
   a. There were laws which were unfair to Japanese and Chinese.

b. Japanese are very smart.

c. Dr. Noguchi hated Japan.

d. Dr. Noguchi was not allowed to study in America.

5. Which of the following was mentioned *first* in the story?

   a. Dr. Noguchi traveled a great deal.

   b. Dr. Noguchi came to America.

   c. Dr. Noguchi was injured but recovered.

   d. Dr. Noguchi worked in South America.

6. The word *crippled* (paragraph 3) means:

   a. lost.   **c.** discovered.

   b. cured.   **d.** useless.

7. The word *adopted* (paragraph 5) means:

   a. took as your own.   **c.** purchased.

   b. denied.   **d.** destroyed.

8. A *poor* title for this story would be:

   a. A Famous Scientist.

   b. The Japanese Who Wanted to Be an American Citizen.

   c. A Man Who Overcame His Problems.

   d. Yellow Fever in South America.

Discovering

Fun with Words: Crossword Puzzle

Copy the crossword puzzle in your notebook. Then fill in the white boxes with the correct words.

If you do not know how to do crossword puzzles, check with your teacher or someone in the class who knows how to do them. They are fun to do. Try this one and you'll see what we mean.

Across

1. snakes' teeth (para. 1)
4. all people (para. 7)
7. to make an effort (para. 4)
8. took as your own (para. 5)
9. Dr. Noguchi's first name
10. initials meaning doctor

Down

1. to remain still (para. 1)
2. given (para. 7)
3. able to (para. 1)
5. a solution (para. 6)
6. made up your mind (para. 3)
8. also (para. 4)

Discovering

Find Out More

1. Dr. Noguchi could not become an American citizen because there were laws that kept Japanese and Chinese from becoming citizens. Are these laws still in effect?

   Write to the Federal immigration office of your state and inquire about this. Share your findings with your teacher. Don't spoil the secret for your classmates.

2. Dr. Noguchi worked on many serious diseases. Find out more about them and write a report to share with your teacher. You can look in any encyclopedia or health book. Here are some ideas:
   a. Rocky Mountain Fever
   b. Yellow Fever
   c. Trachoma

"Good-for-Nothing"

Medal Winner

He wrote and drew children's books.
Millions of people love his Madeline.
Who was this man?

"Stop that drawing," shouted the teacher. "You will grow up to be a good-for-nothing."

Young *Ludwig Bemelmans* looked sadly out of the window. He loved to draw and paint. He painted pictures of the Austrian Mountains. He also loved to invent funny characters and make up stories.

"This is such foolishness," his teachers would say. "Young German men must study something important."

Ludwig quit school. He had to work very hard to make a living. He had all sorts of jobs. At

night, he would go to his hotel room and paint.
One day, he decided to leave Germany. He would
go to America. Perhaps, there he could paint
and write.

He was only 16 when he came to America.
Again, he spent his days working. At night, he
wrote stories and painted. He was lucky and
got jobs illustrating books. Yet his real dream
was to write and illustrate his own books.

All of his books had a certain charm. People
enjoyed them but nobody thought they would
sell. Then in 1934, one of his books, *Hansi,* was
published. Another book was published in 1935

and two more in 1937. Before long, five of his children's books had been published. He also wrote five books for adults.

Madeline was born in the late 1930's. She was a little girl in a book by Bemelmans. Everyone loved her. Children liked to hear about Madeline again and again.

In 1953, he wrote his most famous book. Again, it was about Madeline. It was called *Madeline's Rescue.* More people than ever loved it. It won a gold medal. It became the most famous children's book of 1953.

Ludwig Bemelmans had done it. His dream of writing and painting had come true. Bemelmans loved America, and America loved his books. This German-American gave us all a gift. *Madeline* will be enjoyed by children forever.

Remembering

1. Which one of the following best states the *main idea* of paragraph 8? (Reread the paragraph.)
   a. *Madeline's Rescue* won a gold medal.
   b. *Madeline's Rescue* was the best book of 1953.
   c. In 1953, Bemelmans wrote his most famous book.
   d. More people than ever loved the book.

2. Which one or more of the following are *facts* presented in the story?
   a. Bemelmans drew funny characters.
   b. Bemelmans lived in Germany as a boy.
   c. Bemelmans only wrote and drew children's books.
   d. Bemelmans was 18 when he came to America.

3. Which one or more of the following are *facts* presented in the story?
   a. Bemelmans refused to work.
   b. Bemelmans did not want to come to America.
   c. *Madeline* was not accepted at first.
   d. Bemelmans won a gold medal.

4. Even though *it doesn't say so* in the story, you can tell that:
   a. Germans are not allowed to write.
   b. Bemelmans liked to sing.

    c. Bemelmans had a sister named Madeline.

    d. Teachers are sometimes wrong.

5. Which one of the following was mentioned *first* in the story?

    a. Bemelmans painted pictures of the mountains.

    b. Bemelmans decided to leave Germany.

    c. Bemelman's first book about Madeline was written.

    d. Bemelmans got a job illustrating books.

6. The word *illustrating* (paragraph 5) means:

    a. writing and correcting a book.

    b. printing a book.

    c. drawing pictures for a book.

    d. trying to sell a book.

7. The word *characters* (paragraph 2) means:

    a. big words in a story.

    b. people or animals in a story.

    c. what people say about someone.

    d. a kind of food.

8. A *poor* title for this story would be:

    a. The Birth of *Madeline*.

    b. The Famous Children's Author.

    c. An Artist and Writer of Books.

    d. The Teacher's Dream Comes True.

Discovering

Fun with Words: Be a Word Detective

See if you can find the word that best fits each of the following. Try timing yourself to see how quickly (but carefully) you can get all the answers.

1. Which word means "to make up; to create"? (para. 2)
2. Which word means "grown-ups"? (para. 6)
3. Which word means "put into print"? (para. 6)
4. Which word means "maybe"? (para. 4)
5. Which word means "a present"? (para. 9)

Find Out More

1. Find the book *Madeline* or *Madeline's Rescue* at the library. Read it and share it with your little brothers and sisters or friends.

2. Pretend that you are an author of children's books. How would you go about writing a story? One thing to do is to ask children what they like about the stories they now read. Do you think you could write one? Why don't you try? Share your story with others.

Gentle-Hearted Monster

In the movies he scared millions of people.
Behind the scenes he was a kind, warmhearted Santa Claus.

"You cause millions of people to lose sleep. You frighten millions of others. The Frankenstein monster is feared by everyone. That's you, you're Frankenstein," said the scared woman. Then she hurried down the street.

Boris Karloff just smiled. Yes, he played the Frankenstein monster in the movies. But he was really not a monster. He was a gentle, hardworking actor.

Boris Karloff was born in England. When he was twenty-two, he left for Canada. While living in Canada, he worked at odd jobs. At night, he studied acting. He got parts in small plays and shows. He finally decided to move to the United States.

He worked in North Dakota, Chicago, and California. He played hundreds of parts. He did musical comedy, drama, and other plays. Perhaps, he could make it in the movies. He decided to try.

His start was not easy. Karloff could only get parts as an extra. He was always a man in a crowd. Then he got some larger parts, but no one really noticed him. One day, he tried out for the Frankenstein part. He won the part and was on his way to stardom.

The movie was a smash hit. It was followed by three others about the monster. Other horror movies followed. Films about mummies, ghosts, and vampires became popular. Karloff became the big star of these horror films.

Soon horror shows were heard on radio. Again, Karloff was the chief ghost. His scary

voice kept millions awake. The radio show "Lights Out" became very popular. Everyone knew who Boris Karloff was. He was now an international horror star. When horror shows came on television, Karloff came with them. He seemed to be able to frighten people best.

At home, Karloff was anything but a monster. He enjoyed books, music, and his family. On Christmas, he played Santa Claus for crippled children. This great actor has entertained millions. Both English and Americans may be frightened by his monster roles, but they are also proud of him.

Remembering

1. Which one of the following best states the *main idea* of paragraph 5? (Reread the paragraph.)
   a. Karloff played extra parts.
   b. Karloff appeared as a man in a crowd.
   c. Karloff got a chance to try out for the monster.
   d. Karloff's start in movies was not easy.

2. Which one or more of the following are *facts* presented in the story?
   a. Karloff was born in England.
   b. Karloff was a hard worker.
   c. Karloff lived in Canada.
   d. Karloff lived in Mexico.

3. Which one or more of the following are *facts* presented in the story?
   a. Karloff played the *Mummy*.
   b. Karloff did radio horror shows.
   c. Karloff never appeared on television.
   d. Karloff never played non-horror parts.

4. Even though *it doesn't say so* in the story, you can tell that:
   a. Karloff liked to frighten people, even when he wasn't acting.
   b. Actors are often different from the people they play in movies.

c. Karloff appeared in only one monster movie.

d. Karloff did not have any children of his own.

5. Which of the following was mentioned *first* in the story?
   a. Karloff did horror shows on radio.
   b. Karloff moved to Canada.
   c. Karloff played Santa Claus.
   d. Karloff played the role of Frankenstein.

6. The word *extra* (paragraph 5) means:
   a. one actor who is not needed.
   b. an actor with a very small part.
   c. a member of a gang.
   d. a person who helps the director.

7. The word *horror* (paragraph 6) means:
   a. frightening; scary.
   b. entertaining.
   c. shown in the evening.
   d. easy to make.

8. A *poor* title for this story would be:
   a. The Man Who Played Monsters.
   b. Life of a Canadian Actor.
   c. The Man Who Frightened Millions.
   d. The Many Faces of Boris Karloff.

Discovering

Fun with Words: Crossword Puzzle

Copy the crossword puzzle into your notebook. Then fill in the white boxes with the correct words.

If you do not know how to do crossword puzzles, check with your teacher or someone in the class who knows how to do them. They are fun to do. Try this one and you'll see what we mean.

Across
1. monsters (para. 6)
3. staying in a place (para. 3)
6. a success (para. 6)
7. leading actor (para. 6)

Down
1. large numbers (para. 7)
2. films (para. 2)
4. opposite of day (para. 3)
5. man who is in movies (para. 2)

Discovering

Find Out More

1. Do you know the story of Frankenstein? Find a book on him, and read about him. Share the story with the class.

2. Find out what famous actor played Count Dracula. Who played the Wolfman?

3. Do you know how the faces of actors are made to look like monsters? How do they do it? See if you can find out. Make your own monster mask. If you need help you can:
   a. Look up "make-up" in an encyclopedia.
   b. See your art teacher for ideas.
   c. Ask your teacher to work with you.

61

A Gift of Gold

*The first time he tried New York he failed.
The next time, he became a great star.*

Robert did not always want to sing. His father would tell him that he was wasting a gift. Everyone told him he had a beautiful voice. It was like a gift of gold. Mr. Goulet (goo LAY) was a devout French-Canadian Catholic. He believed that such gifts should be appreciated.

So he trained his son's voice. He wanted him to sing in the church choir. In Canada, this was an honor. Even though they now lived in the United States, Mr. Goulet still wanted his son to sing.

When Robert was 14, his father died. The family returned to Canada. Robert completed his schooling there. He also began his career in show business. He started out as a disc jockey. During his off hours, he continued studying acting and singing. He even won a scholarship to a music conservatory in Toronto.

During this time, he appeared in small shows. He sang minor roles in musicals. He also made a few brief television appearances. His start was modest, but it was a start.

In 1954, he decided to try making it on Broadway. This was tough. Parts in shows were scarce. Jobs were few. He had to work in a department store to make money for food. *Robert Goulet* decided to give up on New York. He returned to Toronto a failure.

He was down, but he didn't quit. He got a couple of parts in shows. These led to other roles. Before long, he became a regular on Canadian daytime television. Fan mail came in by the thousands. Robert Goulet had become a Canadian star. In fact, he was voted Canada's best television singer for three years in a row.

Now Broadway came looking for him! He was given a lead role in *Camelot,* a musical play. He became recognized as the outstanding star in the show. His voice and handsome looks captured the hearts of millions.

In no time, Goulet was an international star. He received as much as $10,000 for one performance. Women fainted when he came on stage. Men were jealous of his voice and good looks. He got offers to make movies and to appear on television.

This Canadian-American proved himself a great star. His talent has enriched both Canadians and Americans. He has helped bring the two nations even closer. Both Canadians and Americans can take great pride in his success.

Remembering

1. Which one of the following best states the *main idea* of paragraph 6? (Reread the paragraph.)
   a. Goulet got small parts in shows.
   b. Goulet was a failure, but he didn't give up.
   c. Goulet got a chance on television shows.
   d. Goulet became Canada's best television singer.

2. Which one or more of the following are *facts* presented in the story?
   a. Goulet made it his first time on Broadway.
   b. Goulet sang in the church choir.
   c. Mr. Goulet discouraged Robert's singing.
   d. Robert studied in Toronto.

3. Which one or more of the following are *facts* presented in the story?
   a. Goulet worked in a department store.
   b. The Goulets returned to Canada when Robert was 14.
   c. Goulet became an international star.
   d. Goulet appeared in a show titled *Camelot.*

4. Even though *it doesn't say so* in the story, you can tell that:
   a. Goulet likes the United States more than Canada.
   b. Becoming a star is not easy.

    c. Goulet never made much money.

    d. *Camelot* was written by a Canadian.

5. Which one of the following was mentioned *first* in the story?

    a. Goulet worked in a department store.

    b. Goulet studied in Toronto.

    c. Goulet received $10,000 for one performance.

    d. Goulet worked as a disc jockey.

6. The word *minor* (paragraph 4) means:

    a. important.

    b. small or unimportant.

    c. paying a lot of money.

    d. having to do with a child.

7. The word *scarce* (paragraph 5) means:

    a. difficult.

    b. unimportant.

    c. hard to get.

    d. low paying.

8. A *poor* title for this story would be:

    a. Canada's Television Idol.

    b. The Boy in the Choir.

    c. A French-Canadian Charmer.

    d. The Man Who Never Quit.

Discovering

Fun with Words: Scramble

Below are five words from the story. They are scrambled. See if you can figure out what each scrambled word is. Write the words in your notebook. Try to do it without looking back. If you can't, look back.

1. ywrdbaao (para. 5)
2. smvoie (para. 8)
3. ntrntnlieaioa (para. 8)
4. llmnsioi (para. 7)
5. gstea (para. 8)

Find Out More

1. Now that you have learned about Robert Goulet, talk to your parents or grandparents. See what they know about him.
   a. Do they know where he was born?
   b. Do they know his ethnic background?
   c. Is he still singing? Where does he live?

2. Robert Goulet has made many records. Do you have one at home? If not, try to get one and listen to it. How do you like his singing? What do your friends think?

Dr. Mays: Slave's Son

Maybe he was a slave's son, but he became Martin Luther King's teacher.

Little *Benjamin Mays* watched. He began to cry. Why were these white men hurting his father? Why did they make him take off his hat and bow down? Why were they making fun of this man he loved so dearly? Was it because he was a former slave? Later, he asked his father these questions. All his father said was, "Do you want me to get lynched?" As a child, Benjamin lived with the fear of being hanged by a group of angry Georgia whites.

It was uncommon in 1900 for a former slave's son to make friends with a former master's son. But Benjamin became the white boy's friend. He learned how to read and write. He felt that with an education he could help change the life of all blacks. He left the South, determined to go to college.

It was not easy for a black man to get a job. It was even harder to be able to study and pass his college classes. But Benjamin never quit! He had to work hard all day and study at night. One day many years later, Benjamin graduated from college. He had one of the highest degrees a person can get in a university. He was now Dr. Mays, Ph.D., and a church minister. If only his mother and father and those Georgia whites could see him now!

The Georgia whites did see him again, and they never forgot him. Dr. Mays became an author, president of several colleges, and a leader in the world-wide YMCA. He also was an advisor to the President of the United States. He became a leader in the United Nations. He was a leader in the Church of Christ. He was the teacher of Martin Luther King. The son of a slave did all these things and more!

Whites and blacks alike are united in their respect for this great man. But the black man looks with special pride upon the accomplishments of his brother. For even though Benjamin became famous and important, he was always proud to be black. He always held his head high. He never quit on himself or his people.

Remembering

1. Which one of the following best states the *main idea* of paragraph 3? (Reread the paragraph.)
   a. It was hard for Mays to get a job.
   b. Studying was hard for Mays.
   c. Mays became a church minister.
   d. Mays worked hard to succeed.

2. Which one or more of the following are *facts* presented in the story?
   a. Benjamin disliked his parents.
   b. Some Georgia whites were cruel.
   c. Benjamin was ashamed of being black.
   d. Benjamin was a leader in the United Nations.

3. Which one or more of the following are *facts* presented in the story?
   a. Benjamin's father was a former slave.
   b. Benjamin went to college in the South.
   c. Benjamin advised a President.
   d. Martin Luther King was Benjamin's student.

4. Even though *it doesn't say so* in the story, you can tell that:
   a. Mays had a lot of courage.
   b. Slaves' sons are not smart.
   c. Most slaves were lazy.
   d. Dr. Mays did not like the President of the United States.

73

Remembering

5. Which of the following was mentioned *first* in the story?
   a. Mays became a leader in the Church of Christ.
   b. Mays became the friend of the white master's son.
   c. Mays left Georgia to go to college.
   d. Mays wrote many books.

6. The word *advisor* (paragraph 4) means:
   a. someone who helps you make decisions.
   b. someone who gives you money.
   c. someone who rules you.
   d. someone who needs help.

7. The word *accomplishments* (paragraph 5) means:
   a. things that have been done well.
   b. accidents.
   c. understandings.
   d. partners.

8. A *poor* title for this story would be:
   a. A Man Who Never Quit.
   b. A Great Entertainer.
   c. A Famous Black Teacher.
   d. A Man of Many Accomplishments.

Discovering

Fun with Words: Fill In

In the story you will find words that can be used to fill the blanks in the sentences below. See if you can get all of them right. You may look back in the story if you wish. Write the words in your notebook.

The life of a slave was not an easy one. At any moment he might be captured by an angry mob and _____ from a tree. The law did
_(para. 1)
not even help him. Many sheriffs seemed _____
_(para. 2)
_____ to let the mob do what it wanted.

The children of slaves also had a hard time. They could not go to school. The only _____
_(para. 2)
that they got was the little that their parents could teach them. None of them _____ from
_(para. 3)
school as white children did. They could receive no _____ from universities.
_(para. 3)

It is no wonder that slaves had to work hard to keep their self-respect. It is difficult to feel _____ when you live in fear.
_(para. 5)

Find Out More

One important accomplishment of Benjamin Mays was not mentioned in this story. In 1963 he went to another country for a very special reason. See if you can find out why.

Vocabulary Review

STORIES 6-10

Following are some of the words you learned in the stories you have read. See if you can remember what these words mean. Try your hardest. Write your answers in your notebook.

1. *Crippled* means:
   a) cured. **b)** lost. **c)** useless. **d)** discovered.

2. *Adopted* means:
   a) purchased. **b)** destroyed. **c)** denied. **d)** took as your own.

3. *Illustrating* means:
   a) writing. **b)** printing. **c)** drawing. **d)** selling.

4. *Characters* means:
   a) words. **b)** people or animals. **c)** talk.
   d) foods.

5. *Extra* means:
   a) one actor who is not needed.

b) an actor with a small part. **c)** a member of a gang. **d)** a person who helps the director.

6. *Horror* means:
   a) frightening. **b)** entertaining. **c)** shown in the dark. **d)** easy to make.

7. *Minor* means:
   a) important. **b)** small or unimportant. **c)** a movie part that pays lots of money. **d)** having to do with a king.

8. *Scarce* means:
   a) difficult. **b)** unimportant. **c)** hard to get. **d)** low paying.

9. *Advisor* means:
   a) someone who helps you make decisions.
   b) someone who needs help.
   rules you. **d)** someone who gives you money.

10. *Accomplishments* means:
    a) fears. **b)** understandings. **c)** things that have been done well. **d)** partners.

One-Man Team

One man isn't the whole team.
But this man made his team a powerhouse.

With the wind in his face, the young Indian found joy in running and jumping over fallen trees. There were few schools for American Indians around 1900. So *Jim Thorpe* spent his time fishing, hunting, and swimming. His body was strong and hard. He could run and jump like a deer.

Many people felt that Indians who wanted to should be able to go to school. These people started schools for Indians. Jim began to realize that an education was important. He wanted to go to school. He got his chance when he was admitted to the Carlisle Indian School in Pennsylvania. He learned to read and write.

But he loved sports best. He quickly became a star in baseball, track, wrestling, lacrosse (luh KRAWS), and football. His school team became a powerhouse. Tiny Carlisle began playing big universities like Harvard and West Point.

In 1912, Jim Thorpe was selected for the U.S. Olympic team. He was asked to take part in the pentathlon (pen TATH lun) and the decathlon (dee KATH lun). These two events required fantastic ability and strength. The pentathlon had five events, including the 200 meter dash, discus throw, and javelin throw. The decathlon had ten events, including the 400 meter dash, pole vault, shot put, and hurdles. No one believed any man could do all these events. Jim Thorpe won a gold medal in both! The whole world was amazed. Jim Thorpe, an Indian, was America's greatest hero!

Then a sad thing happened. Before the Olympics, Jim had once played baseball for a few dollars a game. When you get paid for sports, you are considered a professional. Professionals cannot play in the Olympics. It was decided that Thorpe had to return his gold medals.

Many people believed this was very unfair.
He had only played a few games and got very
little money. But the medals were still taken back.
    At first, Jim was going to give up sports.
Then he decided to become a professional
football player. He was soon the greatest player

in the game. But he never forgot about losing
his gold medals. He felt he had been cheated.

In 1950, three years before his death, he was
named the outstanding athlete of modern times.
This great honor brought pride to his people. He
will always be remembered as one of the world's
greatest all-around athletes.

Remembering

1. Which one of the following best states the *main idea* of paragraph 1? (Reread the paragraph.)
   a. Jim Thorpe could fish, hunt, run, and swim.
   b. Thorpe did not go to school.
   c. Jim Thorpe developed his strength and speed instead of going to school.
   d. Jim Thorpe liked to run.

2. Which one or more of the following are *facts* presented in the story?
   a. Jim was a professional golfer.
   b. Jim won the decathlon and pentathlon.
   c. Jim Thorpe attended Harvard College.
   d. Jim did not like school.

3. Which one or more of the following are *facts* presented in the story?
   a. Jim won a gold medal in archery.
   b. Jim played professional football.
   c. Jim felt he had been cheated in the Olympics.
   d. Thorpe did not mind losing his gold medals.

4. Even though *it doesn't* say so in the story, you can tell that:
   a. The Olympics are held every five years.
   b. The pentathlon is very difficult.
   c. Thorpe knew that he was not allowed to be in the Olympics.
   d. All Indians were able to go to school in 1900.

5. Which of the following was mentioned *first* in the story?
   a. Jim attended the Carlisle School in Pennsylvania.
   b. Thorpe was named the outstanding athlete of modern times.
   c. Thorpe lost his gold medals.
   d. Jim became a professional football player.

6. The word *admitted* (paragraph 2) means:
   a. provided.
   b. supported.
   c. recognized.
   d. let in.

7. The word *powerhouse* (paragraph 3) means:
   a. someone who is very rich.
   b. a storehouse.
   c. something that is very strong.
   d. someone who is very pretty.

8. A *poor* title for this story would be:
   a. A Famous American Indian.
   b. The 1912 Olympics.
   c. An All-Around Athlete.
   d. An Olympic Hero.

Discovering

Fun with Words: Be a Word Detective

See if you can find the word that best fits each of the following. Try timing yourself to see how quickly (but carefully) you can get all the answers.

1. Which word means "a graceful animal"? (para. 1)
2. Which word means "unbelievable; great"? (para. 4)
3. Which word is another name for colleges? (para. 3)
4. Which word is the name of the international sports contests? (para. 5)
5. Which word means "an award for winning"? (para. 4)

Find Out More

1. The decathlon has 10 events in it. We named only a few. Can you find out what all the 10 events are? Look up "Olympics" or "decathlon" in an encyclopedia or a dictionary. Write the list in your notebook. Don't give away your secret.

2. The Olympics are held in a different country every four years. Do you know what country they will be held in next? Where could you look to find out?

3. Go to a track meet at your school. How many events do you recognize from the story?

White House Advisor

She was only a sharecropper's daughter. She later became the advisor to many American Presidents.

The little black girl hid behind a tree. She sadly watched the white children enter school. How she wished she could go to school! Mary wanted so much to learn reading and writing, but for her, school was only a dream. In 1882, there were few schools for black children in the South. Little *Mary Bethune* had to work. She was one of seventeen children of sharecropper parents. Day and night, they worked their small farm in South Carolina.

Again and again, Mary asked to go to school. One day, her church minister told her he had found a school for her. She entered Scotia (SKO shuh) Seminary (SEM uh neh ree), a church school in North Carolina. She had a quick mind and studied hard.

Mary studied at Scotia for seven years. She then went on to another church college, Moody Bible Institute. For a time, she considered a career as a missionary. She hoped to go to Africa to spread the Christian religion. Her request was denied. She could not go to Africa.

It was at this time that Mary turned to teaching. She had a special interest in helping educate black women in America. In 1923, she founded the Bethune-Cookman College for Women in Florida. She hoped to help black women gain their rightful place in society. She also realized the need for more national black groups. She had a dream of a council that would unite all black groups and enable them to work for one common purpose. As a result of this dream, she established the National Council of Negro Women. Today it has over one million members.

Because of her work with black women and youth, Mary became well known. Soon even the President of the United States heard of her. She became advisor to President Hoover during the Depression. She later counseled President Franklin D. Roosevelt. She was the only black woman in Roosevelt's "Black Cabinet." This was a group of advisors on black affairs. Under Roosevelt, she became head of a new agency, the Division of Negro Affairs.

Later, Dr. Bethune was one of President Truman's official advisors who went to San Francisco for the start of the United Nations.

In 1955 shortly before her death, she was awarded the Springarn Medal by the NAACP. This medal is given to the person who has done the most for blacks. It was well deserved by this woman. For nearly eighty years, Mary Bethune had dedicated herself to bettering the life of all black Americans.

Remembering

1. Which one of the following best states the *main idea* of paragraph 5? (Reread the paragraph.)
   a. Mary Bethune advised President Hoover.
   b. Mary Bethune helped her county.
   c. Mary Bethune served under President Roosevelt.
   d. Mary Bethune was the only woman in the "Black Cabinet."

2. Which one or more of the following are *facts* presented in the story?
   a. Mary Bethune wanted to be a missionary to Africa.
   b. Bethune College was located in Maryland.
   c. Mary Bethune founded the NAACP.
   d. Mary Bethune knew Presidents Kennedy and Nixon.

3. Which one or more of the following are *facts* presented in the story?
   a. Mary worked as a waitress.
   b. Mary's application to teach in Africa was denied.
   c. Mary founded a college in Louisiana.
   d. Dr. Bethune went to San Francisco for the start of the United Nations.

4. Even though *it doesn't say so* in the story, you can tell that:
   a. The National Council of Negro Women has gained much influence in America.

Remembering

    b. Mary Bethune was awarded the Nobel Peace Prize.

    c. The life of a sharecropper was easy.

    d. Mary Bethune gave a lot of money to the United Nations.

5. Which one of the following was mentioned first in the story?

    a. Mary Bethune attended a meeting that started the United Nations.

    b. Mary Bethune received the Springarn Award.

    c. Mary hoped to be a missionary.

    d. Mary founded the Bethune-Cookman College for black women.

6. The word *founded* (paragraph 4) means:

    a. started.   **c.** made bigger.

    b. discovered.   **d.** bought.

7. The word *denied* (paragraph 3) means:

    a. accepted.   **c.** permitted.

    b. refused.   **d.** recognized.

8. A *poor* title for this story would be:

    a. A Woman Who Helped Her People.

    b. A Dedicated Educator.

    c. The African Missionary.

    d. A Great Black Woman.

Discovering

Fun with Words: Crossword Puzzle

Copy the crossword puzzle into your notebook. Then fill in the white boxes with the correct words.

Across
1. kind of school (para. 2)
4. large number (para. 4)
5. to teach (para. 4)
6. all the people (para. 4)
7. leader of a nation (para. 5)
8. set of beliefs (para. 3)

Down
1. farmer who does not own land (para. 1)
2. people in an organization (para. 4)
3. every (para. 4)

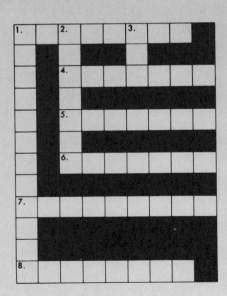

Discovering

Find Out More

1. As stated in the story, Dr. Bethune established Bethune-Cookman College. From any source, see if you can find out how the college operates today. Try to find out how many students attend. Is it still a black college open to women only?

2. The twenty-second amendment to the Constitution was passed because of something that happened to one of the Presidents whom Mary Bethune advised. See if you can find out what this amendment says. Who was the President? What was different about his Presidency?

Blind Inspiration

He was blind from birth.
But when he played his guitar and sang,
you knew his soul did not need eyes.

"Mrs. Feliciano (feh lee see AH no), you have a fine son," said the nurse.

The woman lying in the bed smiled. "José is what we shall name him," she thought. Then she fell asleep.

Several weeks later, a sad thing was discovered. Young José was blind. What will become of him? How will he be treated? What can a blind person do? All of these questions worried José's mother and father. In time, there were seven brothers in his home. His father worked hard on their farm in Puerto Rico. Money was a problem. Feeding the children was also a problem. But *José Feliciano* was not a problem. As a young child, he began to learn to play the guitar. He worked hard at it, and he learned very fast. He seemed to have a gift for music. His playing and singing helped make his family happy.

One day José's father decided to try for a better life in New York. The family moved to New York City. They soon discovered that life was even harder there. Only low-paying jobs were offered to them. But the Feliciano family never lost hope. Everyone helped support the family, even José!

When he was thirteen, José would play his guitar in Greenwich Village. People enjoyed his playing and singing. They gave him money. Everyone enjoyed his music, and they encouraged the talented blind guitarist. José worked even harder at his music. He learned to play the organ, bongos, banjo, bass, and other instruments. He had decided to make his living in music.

He was only seventeen when he got his first nightclub job in Detroit. Before long, José was entertaining in nightclubs all over the United States. He became a favorite of Spanish-speaking people and all other Americans. Everyone sensed that his music came right from his heart and soul.

Then one day, a man from a record company signed José to a recording contract. This was a big chance for him. He wondered whether he could make it. He made it, and made it big! In 1968, he won two Grammy awards. He received one as the outstanding male artist. He won a second as the outstanding new artist of the year. These awards proved that José was a star.

Since then, José has made several albums that have sold over one million copies each. He appears on television and in movies and is heard

on the radio. The blind boy everyone worried
about became rich and famous. But he did not
forget either his family or others who are
handicapped.

José bought a farm in Puerto Rico for his
family. He makes many charity appearances to
help the blind. He frequently visits hospitals to
encourage people who are sick or handicapped.
His hard work and success are an inspiration to
Puerto Ricans and other minorities. In fact, his
life can be an inspiration to all people.

Remembering

1. Which one of the following best states the *main idea* of paragraph 7? (Reread the paragraph.)
   a. José was signed to a record company contract.
   b. José became a recording star.
   c. José won a Grammy award.
   d. One Grammy was for the outstanding male performer of 1968.

2. Which one or more of the following are *facts* presented in the story?
   a. José was born in New York City.
   b. José was thirteen when he won a Grammy award.
   c. José played many musical instruments.
   d. José was one of three children in his family.

3. Which one or more of the following are *facts* presented in the story?
   a. José's family returned to Puerto Rico.
   b. José attended college to study music.
   c. Spanish-speaking people like José's records.
   d. None of José's albums have sold over one million copies.

4. Even though *it doesn't say so* in the story, you can tell that:
   a. Puerto Rican people are good musicians.
   b. It is easy to learn to play the guitar.

    c. Blind people can succeed.

    d. José's family did not want him to be a musician.

5. Which one of the following was mentioned *first* in the story?

    a. Seven brothers were born to the family.

    b. José sang in Greenwich Village.

    c. José won a Grammy award.

    d. José was found to be blind.

6. The word *handicapped* (paragraph 8) means:

    a. having an unusual problem or condition.

    b. unusually strong.

    c. without talent.

    d. not living in the big city.

7. The word *inspiration* (paragraph 9) means:

    a. a show-off.

    b. something that makes you want to try.

    c. someone who makes you worry.

    d. a poor example for others to follow.

8. A *poor* title for this story would be:

    a. A Sad Puerto Rican Farmer.

    b. The Blind Grammy Winner.

    c. The Star from Puerto Rico.

    d. A Great Guitarist.

Discovering

Fun with Words: Scramble

Here are some words from the story. They are scrambled. See if you can figure out what each word is. Be on your toes.

1. ttdraee (para. 3)
2. eeeetsvnn (para. 6)
3. blaums (para. 8)
4. spnrtniiaoi (para. 9)
5. edsidvocre (para. 3)

Find Out More

1. See if anyone in your class has a record by José Feliciano. Bring the record in and share it with the class. You might want to write to Mr. Feliciano in care of his record company. You can tell him you enjoy his records. See if he replies to your letter.

2. A handicap does not have to prevent an individual from enjoying life or from becoming a success. Read about some other famous handicapped people who became very successful and led rewarding lives. For example, read about Helen Keller and Ray Charles.

3. Do you know any blind people? How do you feel when you see a blind person on the street? What is it like to be blind? Discuss these questions with your class.

Fame and Freedom

*Even as a child she stuck by her beliefs.
Later in life her beliefs would cost her
a career and her fortune.*

Little Melina was only five. Yet she loved the exciting Greek music. She loved to dance on tables. It was not often that she sat still. She was like a gypsy. But her father was often embarrassed.

Mr. Mercouri was a member of the Greek government. He was also very wealthy. Many government officials visited his home. There were visitors from other lands who spoke different languages. They had different ways of life. Many different customs became known to the Mercouri family. This way of life was exciting for Melina. It also made her parents very concerned about her behavior.

Melina Mercouri continued to love dancing and acting. As she grew older, her parents became worried. They thought her interests were not proper. A government official's daughter should not act on the stage. But Melina had a mind of her own. She was determined to become an actress. She left home and went to acting school.

Her natural talent was unbelievable. In no time, she was playing many roles. She did comedy and musicals. She seemed to be able to act any part.

Before long, she began making Greek movies. Her films were successful in Greece. However, few people knew her outside Greece. Then one day, she had a chance for international stardom.

A French director had seen her in a movie. He was planning to make a movie about a Greek woman. He felt Melina was perfect for the role. She agreed to play the part. The movie became an international hit. Melina Mercouri won many awards for her role. Many people felt she deserved an academy award in Hollywood. She did not win one, however.

Melina was now as popular in New York as she was in Athens. She made movies and television appearances and appeared in plays.

Then in 1967, Greece was taken over by the Greek military. The king was sent out of the country. Greece's regular laws and freedoms

were suspended. Freedom of speech and press were also taken away. Freedom-loving Greeks were forced to leave the country. Those who remained risked being jailed.

Melina Mercouri fled Greece. She gave up her home and career for her beliefs. She came to the United States. From America, she helped raise money. She spoke out against the dictators in her country. She tried to get help for her people.

In 1974, there was again a change in the Greek government. The military gave up its control of the country. Many Greeks returned to their homeland. Melina returned with them. She had never given up hope for her country's freedom. Her father would have been proud.

Remembering

1. Which one of the following best states the *main idea* of paragraph 4? (Reread the paragraph.)
   a. Melina could act in musicals.
   b. Melina performed in old Greek plays.
   c. Melina was good at comedy.
   d. Melina's talent was unbelievable.

2. Which one or more of the following are *facts* presented in the story?
   a. Melina's father was a government official.
   b. Melina's home was visited by people from other countries.
   c. Melina won an Academy Award.
   d. Melina's father wanted her to act on the stage.

3. Which one or more of the following are *facts* presented in the story?
   a. Melina played in movies.
   b. Melina returned to Greece in 1974.
   c. Greece was taken over by the Greek army.
   d. Melina became an international star.

4. Even though *it doesn't say so* in the story, you can tell that:
   a. The daughters of many Greek officials are famous actresses.
   b. Melina cannot speak English.
   c. Melina loves Greece, her homeland.
   d. The Greek military tried to find Melina in the United States.

5. Which one of the following was mentioned *first* in the story?
   a. Melina went to acting school.
   b. Melina lived in the United States.
   c. Melina danced on tables.
   d. Melina made Greek movies.

6. The word *officials* (paragraph 2) means:
   a. members of the secret police.
   b. the king and queen.
   c. important government people.
   d. people from universities.

7. The word *suspended* (paragraph 8) means:
   a. taken away.
   b. changed.
   c. enforced.
   d. voted for by the people.

8. A *poor* title for this story would be:
   a. A Greek Patriot.
   b. The Angry Greek Father.
   c. The International Star.
   d. Making of a Star.

Discovering

Fun with Words: Match Meanings

See if you can match the words in Column A with the correct meanings in Column B.

Column A

1. international
2. dictators
3. military
4. stardom
5. gypsy

Column B

a. the army, navy, and other forces
b. fame; popularity
c. a person who travels from place to place
d. world-wide
e. making movies
f. people who have complete control over a country

Find Out More

Do you know what life is like in countries under the rule of a dictatorship? How would you find out about such countries?

Here are some suggestions to help you:

a. Look in magazines and newspapers.
b. Look in your card catalog in the library.
c. Ask your parents and others for suggestions.
d. Try to find out if there are films in your school that show the differences between a democracy and a dictatorship.

Nat Love,

If a black man couldn't make it in the South,
maybe he could make it in the West. This one did.

It was a cattle stampede! The thundering
hooves shook the earth. Many cattle would be
killed if something wasn't done. *Nat Love* was the
first cowboy to realize what was happening. He
tried to head off the stampede. He rode his
horse toward the front of the herd. By firing his
gun and skillfully turning his pony, he turned
the herd toward the river. One slip and he would
be trampled. The hooves of the cattle would crush
him. Luckily, the herd was turned and the
stampede halted.

That evening around the chuckwagon,
everyone told Nat how brave he was. He just
smiled. He had been plenty scared. But Deadwood
Dick, as he was known, had learned to live
with fear.

Cowboy

He had lived with fear as a boy. American slaves were supposed to be freed after the Civil War. But, in Tennessee, Nat's parents were still treated like slaves. Nat decided he would head west. He would not let being black hold him back! At the age of fifteen, in 1869, Nat set out. He was afraid, but his fear did not stop him.

During his first years in Texas and Wyoming, Nat became an expert horseman. He learned to break broncos. He learned how to race like the wind. He became very friendly with Indians. As a black man, he understood how it felt to be mistreated. The Indians adopted him into their tribe. He was like a son of the chief.

But Nat wanted more adventure. He left his Indian friends. A little later, he rode with Billy the Kid. And later he rode with another famous outlaw, Jesse James. It was during this time that Nat became known as "Deadwood Dick."

But the life of an outlaw was not the life for Nat. He did not like breaking the law. He gave up that kind of life and became a cowboy. For many years, he drove cattle on the long trail from Texas to Kansas. During this time, he met many famous people, including Buffalo Bill Cody.

As he grew older, Nat realized that cowboy life was for younger men. He left the range. He wrote a book about his life called *The Life and Adventures of Nat Love.* The only job he could get was as a railroad porter. This was the best job black men could get at that time. People who saw him on a train never realized who he was. Who would have believed that the old porter was Deadwood Dick?

Remembering

1. Which one of the following best states the *main idea* of paragraph 4? (Reread the paragraph.)
   a. Nat was adopted by an Indian tribe.
   b. Nat learned to do many exciting things.
   c. Nat learned how to ride.
   d. Nat learned how to break broncos.

2. Which one or more of the following are *facts* presented in the story?
   a. Nat lived in Texas and Wyoming.
   b. Indians were unfriendly to blacks.
   c. Nat lived in Alabama as a boy.
   d. Nat rode with Jesse James.

3. Which one or more of the following are *facts* presented in the story?
   a. Nat became known as Indian Joe.
   b. Nat was never an outlaw.
   c. Nat wrote a book about his life.
   d. Nat became a railroad engineer.

4. Even though *it doesn't say so* in the story, you can tell that:
   a. There were many black cowboys.
   b. The Indians did not like Nat.
   c. Cattle stampedes are dangerous.
   d. Black people never write books.

Remembering

5. Which one of the following was mentioned *first* in the story?
   a. Nat became a railroad porter.
   b. The Civil War ended.
   c. Nat wrote a book about his life.
   d. Nat rode with the James gang.

6. The word *trampled* (paragraph 1) means:
   a. bumped.
   b. crushed.
   c. afraid.
   d. pushed.

7. The word *outlaw* (paragraph 5) means:
   a. cowboy.
   b. a person who is a hero.
   c. a person who breaks the law.
   d. a person who helps the police.

8. A *poor* title for this story would be:
   a. Nat Love Rides the Range.
   b. How to Become a Railroad Porter.
   c. The Son of a Slave Who Became a Cowboy.
   d. The Story of Deadwood Dick.

Discovering

Fun with Words: Crossword Puzzle

Copy the crossword puzzle into your notebook. Then fill in the white boxes with the correct words.

Across
1. a fight between two armies (para. 3)
5. a native American (para. 5)
6. related to the word "do" (para. 6)

Down
1. name of a state in the West (para. 4)
2. a kind of transportation (para. 7)
3. took into a family (para. 4)
4. the ground (para. 1)

Discovering

Find Out More

In the Old West, outlaws were hard to catch. Sheriffs were given posters that said "Wanted Dead or Alive." What other things were on these posters? See if you can find out what they looked like. Then draw a wanted poster for Deadwood Dick. Show it to your teacher and classmates.

Vocabulary Review

STORIES 11-15

Following are some of the words you learned in the stories you have read. See if you can remember that these words mean. Try your hardest. Write your answers in your notebook.

1. *Admitted* means:
   a) argued. b) provided. c) recognized. d) let in.

2. *Powerhouse* means:
   a) someone who is handsome. b) someone who is wealthy. c) something that is strong. d) a storeroom.

3. *Founded* means:
   a) discovered. b) started. c) made bigger. d) bought.

4. *Denied* means:
   a) refused. b) accepted. c) permitted. d) recognized.

116

5. *Handicapped* means:
   a) having an unusual problem. **b)** unusually strong. **c)** without great talent. **d)** not living in a big city.

6. *Inspiration* means:
   a) a show off. **b)** something that makes you try. **c)** someone who makes you worry. **d)** a poor example.

7. *Officials* means:
   a) secret police. **b)** the king and queen. **c)** important government people. **d)** people who teach.

8. *Suspended* means:
   a) taken away. **b)** changed. **c)** enforced. **d)** voted for by the people.

9. *Trampled* means:
   a) bumped. **b)** afraid. **c)** crushed. **d)** pushed.

10. *Outlaw* means:
    a) a cowboy. **b)** a person who breaks the law. **c)** a hero. **d)** a person who helps the police.

117

A Dream Come True

As a boy he dreamed he'd be a star football player.
All his life he worked to make his dream come true.

This play is the last of the game. The Cowboys need only one yard. One yard means a touchdown and a victory for the Cowboys. The Bears would lose. The quarterback turns and hands off the ball. It's an end run. Blockers crash into number 51 on defense. But his mighty arms push them away and knock them down. He moves down the line. He would rather die than let the ball carrier score. Down goes another blocker with a crash. Number 51 lowers his shoulder and smashes the ball carrier. The noise of the collision can be heard in the stands. The ball carrier is stopped dead. The Cowboys don't score. The game is saved for the Chicago Bears. The crowd goes wild. Fans swarm onto the field. Everyone is pounding the monstrous linebacker on the back. He is so big he looks like a giant. He is again the hero of the hour.

In the locker room, reporters swarm around him. Everyone wants to listen to him. How can one man be so powerful? How can he make so many tackles? He seems to be unstoppable.

Ball carriers fear him. Blockers try to avoid him. Some say he is one of the greatest linebackers of all time. Who is this great star?

Dick Butkus was born in 1942 near Chicago, Illinois. His father, an electrician, had come to America from Lithuania (lith uh WAY nee uh). His mother's parents were also Lithuanian immigrants. His four brothers were all big and tough. They were football players, too. When he was a kid helping them with their equipment, Dick knew football was his game. He loved football. He dreamed he would be a star.

The young man worked to make his dream come true. He lifted weights. He ran. He took jobs that would help to make him stronger. By the time he was in high school, he was a star. Many colleges tried to lure him, but Dick wanted to stay in Illinois. He went to Illinois University. Butkus helped make the Illinois team a winner. One year they won the Big Ten crown. They went to the Rose Bowl and beat Washington State. Butkus was the star of the game. He became an All-American. Only one question was left: Could he make it as a pro football player?

Butkus was drafted by the Chicago Bears. Now he had to win a spot on the team. To win a spot, a man had to be tough, strong, and talented. Again Dick worked day and night. He dedicated himself to making the team. He became a starter during his first year.

Even during his rookie year, Butkus showed his greatness. The Chicago defense was feared

throughout the league. Dick Butkus never quit.
He never let down. Even when he was hurt
he played. He led the team in tackles. He caused
the other team to fumble. He made interceptions.
He was almost a one-man team.

In almost every season as a pro, Butkus
was named to the all-star team. He became the
outstanding defensive player in the league. He
won almost every honor a football player can win.
As a boy, Dick Butkus dreamed one day he'd be
a star. He made his dream come true.

Remembering

1. Which one of the following best states the *main idea* of paragraph 6? (Reread the paragraph.)
   a. Butkus made many unassisted tackles.
   b. Dick frequently caused fumbles.
   c. Dick was almost a one-man team.
   d. Dick played when he was hurt.

2. Which one or more of the following are *facts* presented in the story?
   a. The Chicago Bears beat the Cowboys.
   b. Dick attended Washington University.
   c. Dick's brothers were baseball players.
   d. Butkus played in the Sugar Bowl.

3. Which one or more of the following are *facts* presented in the story?
   a. Dick's father was from Lithuania.
   b. Dick was good but lazy.
   c. Dick became the outstanding defensive player in the league.
   d. Butkus never got hurt playing football.

4. Even though *it doesn't say so* in the story, you can tell that:
   a. Football is a popular game in Lithuania.
   b. Dick did not like Illinois.

   c. Not many pro rookies win a starting job on a team.

   d. Dick was drafted by the Dallas Cowboys.

5. Which one of the following was mentioned *first* in the story?
   a. The Bears signed Butkus.
   b. Dick became an All-American.
   c. Butkus led the team in tackles.
   d. Dick's four brothers played football.

6. The word *monstrous* (paragraph 1) means:
   a. ugly.
   b. very big.
   c. good looking.
   d. beat-up looking.

7. The word *swarm* (paragraph 2) means:
   a. crowd around.
   b. question.
   c. try to get an autograph.
   d. make fun of.

8. A *poor* title for this story would be:
   a. Hard Work Makes Dreams Come True.
   b. Dick Butkus: All-American.
   c. The Chicago Bears, Defensive Star.
   d. A Player Who Made It Just Because He Was Big.

Discovering

Fun with Words: Analogies

Analogies are pairs of words that are related. It is fun to see words in pairs or in related ways. Look at the example. Then see if you can figure out the correct answers by using the words from the story. Work with a partner if you can. Here is an example:

Big is to *little* as *tall* is to:
a) round **b)** heavy **c)** short **d)** flat

The answer is *c, short,* because *little* is the opposite of *big* and *short* is the opposite of *tall.* Try the next few. If you need help, ask your teacher.

1. *Powerful* (para. 2) is to *weak* as *monstrous* (para. 1) is to:
   a) fearless **b)** small **c)** wishful **d)** pretty

2. *Rookie* (para. 6) is to *first-year-man* as *linebacker* (para. 1) is to:
   a) star **b)** defensive back **c)** strong man **d)** outfielder

3. *Chicago Bears* (para. 1) is to *professional team* as *Washington State* (para. 4) is to:
   a) professional team **b)** college team **c)** All-Star team **d)** professional and All-Star team

Discovering

4. *Beat* (para. 4) is to *defeated* as *drafted* (para. 5) is to:

1) warned   **b)** chosen   **c)** punished   **d)** protected

Find Out More

1. A few football words are mentioned in the story. Some of the words are related to offense (when your team has the ball). Other words are related to defense (when your team is trying to stop the other team). Below are two positions mentioned in the story. Can you name other positions on defense or offense? See how many you can come up with. Write the lists in your notebook.

Defense
linebacker

Offense
quarterback

2. Two National Football League (NFL) teams are mentioned in the story. Can you name any more? See how many you can think of. Write the list in your notebook. Score 2 points for each answer. A perfect score is 54 points. How many points can you get?

NFL Teams
(Chicago) Bears
(Dallas) Cowboys

Escape or Die

Nazi Germany was not safe for German Jews.
This is the story of a German who escaped
and came to America.
One day the whole world would know him.

Your family's home, money, business, and
friends are gone! All you have are the clothes
on your back. You are on a boat to a strange
country. How do you feel? You are sad,
frightened, and lonesome. But if you were *Henry
Kissinger,* you would be glad just to be alive!

In Germany, the Nazis had taken over. Every
Jewish family lived in fear. Thousands of
German Jews were being arrested. Their homes
and businesses were being taken away. Some
people said these prisoners were being executed.
Why were they being killed? The only reason
was because they were Jews.

Henry's father realized he and his family
might be next. Maybe they would be arrested

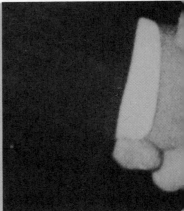

and sent to prison. He decided Germany was
not a safe place for his family. They would have
to leave their beloved homeland. They would
give up their home, money, everything. They
would try to go to America where they had
relatives. In America, they could start a new life.
Fortunately, they were able to escape in 1938.
If they had waited another year, they might never
have gotten out. The Nazis seemed determined
to destroy all German Jews. They killed anyone
trying to leave.

Henry was only sixteen when his family
came to America. He wondered how he would
do in high school. He soon found out. He became
a top student. He had an alert mind and learned
quickly. He graduated from high school and
entered college. In no time, he again became
known as an outstanding student. His teachers

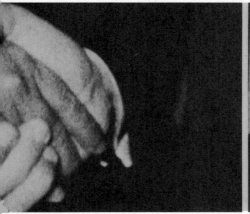

felt Henry would make a good college teacher. This is what he wanted to do, but he had to wait. America was involved in World War II, and Henry wanted to serve his new country. He fought in Germany. By serving his country, he became an American citizen in 1943. Now he was truly a German-American.

After the war, Henry entered Harvard University. He soon finished his studies. He was such a great scholar that he was asked to teach at Harvard. This was a great honor for him. Dr. Kissinger (as he was now known) accepted.

Within a few years, Dr. Kissinger had become known throughout the world. He had written a book about nuclear weapons (atomic bombs and missiles). His book told nations not to use these weapons. Leaders from many countries read his book. They felt Dr. Kissinger's ideas were wise. He traveled to many lands. He advised leaders of many countries. Almost everyone he met liked him and respected his ideas. He seemed to be able to get people to agree on things. He was able to get people to listen to new ideas.

Soon Dr. Kissinger's country again needed his service. In 1969, Dr. Kissinger was made a special advisor to the President. He would advise the President on matters dealing with other nations. This was a most important job. America was involved in the Vietnam War. No one seemed to be able to find a way to end the war. Dr. Kissinger worked on this problem for several years. Finally, a settlement was reached. The war was ended, and American soldiers came home.

People all over the world were thankful the war was over. Dr. Kissinger received world-wide recognition for his efforts. In 1973, he was awarded the Nobel Peace Prize. His hard work was never to be forgotten.

Remembering

1. Which one of the following best states the *main idea* of paragraph 6? (Reread the paragraph.)
   a. Dr. Kissinger became known throughout the world.
   b. Dr. Kissinger wrote a book on atomic weapons.
   c. Dr. Kissinger visited many countries.
   d. Many world leaders respected Kissinger's ideas.

2. Which one or more of the following are *facts* presented in the story?
   a. The Kissingers escaped from Russia.
   b. Henry Kissinger was 16 when he came to America.
   c. Henry studied at Harvard University.
   d. Henry had trouble in high school.

3. Which one or more of the following are *facts* presented in the story?
   a. Dr. Kissinger won the Nobel Prize.
   b. Most of the Jews arrested had murdered someone.
   c. Dr. Kissinger taught at Harvard University.
   d. Kissinger was asked to become President.

4. Even though *it doesn't say so* in the story, you can tell that:
   a. The Kissingers were the last family to leave Germany.
   b. Jews who were killed had committed no crimes.
   c. Henry did not go to school in Germany.
   d. Kissinger wanted the Vietnam War to continue.

Remembering

5. Which one of the following was mentioned *first* in the story?
   a. The Kissingers escaped to America.
   b. Many families were being arrested.
   c. Henry joined the army.
   d. Dr. Kissinger taught at Harvard.

6. The word *executed* (paragraph 2) means:
   a. arrested.
   b. questioned.
   c. sent out of the country.
   d. killed.

7. The word *scholar* (paragraph 5) means:
   a. honest man.
   b. very good student.
   c. teacher.
   d. listener.

8. A *poor* title for this story would be:
   a. The Man Who Helped End the Vietnam War.
   b. The German–American Nobel Prize Winner.
   c. A Man Feared By Many Nations.
   d. The Immigrant Who Advised the President.

Discovering

Fun with Words: Scramble

Below are some of the words from the story. They are scrambled, or all mixed up. See if you can figure out what each word is. Write the words in your notebook. You can look back at the story for clues. Try your hardest!

1. sssnbeui (para. 1)
2. vesretila (para. 3)
3. dgtrauead (para. 4)
4. ccptaede (para. 5)
5. wddraae (para. 8)

Find Out More

1. Do you know what happened to the Nazi leaders after World War II? See if you can find out. Look in an encyclopedia or find a book about them. Report your findings to your class.

2. Crossword puzzles are fun. You have done many of them. Why don't you be the teacher? Use words from this story and make up your own crossword puzzle. Try it out on your friends.

First Lady of Sports

Girls were not supposed to beat boys in sports.
Babe could probably beat most in any sport.

"We don't want Babe to play. She beats all the boys."

Mrs. Didrikson (DEE drik sun) just smiled. She knew her son didn't mean what he said. But it was true. Her daughter Mildred, called "Babe," *was* very good. She could hit a baseball farther. She could throw a football longer. She was the fastest runner. Back in Norway, girls could skate and ski well. But here in America, girls did not play sports. At least some didn't.

Babe Didrikson loved athletics. She learned almost by instinct. She had great natural ability.

135

Until she got to high school, girls laughed at her. Finally, she got to play on a girls' basketball team. In no time, Babe was a star. She even became an All-American. At this time, she was only sixteen years old and 5 feet 4 inches tall!

The 1932 Olympics made Babe an international heroine. During the Olympics, she broke four world records. She broke the record throwing the javelin. She set a new mark in the hurdles. She broke a record for the high jump. All the world heard about Babe.

Babe decided to turn professional. She traveled around the country giving exhibitions. She showed her talent in track, baseball, football, billiards, and other sports. Once, she pitched for the St. Louis Cardinals baseball team. She became even more famous.

The one sport Babe never tried was golf. She decided to try it out. In a very short time, she became a champion golfer. Within a few years, she won the Eastern Women's Open Championship. Later she won the Western Open Championship.

In 1938, Babe married a wrestler named George Zaharias (zuh HAIR ee us). She stopped playing in competition for a while. Each day, she took golf lessons for five or six hours. She was determined to become almost perfect.

In the year 1947, she won 17 straight golf titles. She won them as an amateur. This was because she did not play for money. She now decided to turn pro. In 1953, she won the U.S. National Open. In 1954, she won the All-American

Open. In 1956, Babe became ill and died of
cancer.

Most sports writers and athletes recognize
Babe Zaharias as one of the greatest all-around
athletes of all time. This is including men! She
proved that women could play sports. Thanks to
her, professional women's sports really grew. No
one has ever equaled Babe's all-around talents.

Remembering

1. Which one of the following best states the *main idea* of paragraph 4? (Reread the paragraph.)
   a. Babe broke four world records.
   b. Babe set a world record in hurdles.
   c. The Olympics made Babe a heroine.
   d. Babe broke the record in the javelin throw.

2. Which one or more of the following are *facts* presented in the story?
   a. Babe had talent in billiards.
   b. Babe won the All-American Open.
   c. Babe was over 6 feet tall.
   d. Babe once pitched for the New York Yankees.

3. Which one or more of the following are *facts* presented in the story?
   a. Babe's parents came from Denmark.
   b. Babe had trouble learning golf.
   c. Babe never became a golf professional.
   d. Babe was an All-American basketball player.

4. Even though *it doesn't say so* in the story, you can tell that:
   a. Babe was strong, but she could not run very fast.
   b. Babe was a good basketball player because she was very tall.

Remembering

c. It is very rare for someone to be great in many sports.

d. Babe became a wrestler after she married George Zaharias.

5. Which one of the following was mentioned *first* in the story?
   a. Babe became an All-American.
   b. Babe was in the 1932 Olympics.
   c. Babe won the U.S. Women's Open.
   d. Babe married a wrestler.

6. The word *amateur* (paragraph 8) means:
   a. a very strong athlete.
   b. a beginner in a sport.
   c. a female athlete.
   d. a player who competes for no money.

7. The word *instinct* (paragraph 3) means:
   a. having a good coach.
   b. natural ability.
   c. deciding when to perform.
   d. showing a great skill.

8. A *poor* title for this story would be:
   a. The 1932 Olympics.
   b. The Woman Who Loved Sports.
   c. A Great Golf Champion.
   d. An All-Around Athlete.

Discovering

Fun with Words: Crossword Puzzle

Copy the crossword puzzle into your notebook. Then fill in the white boxes with the correct words.

Across

1. someone who plays for money (para. 8)
3. a house
5. either (para. 7)
6. being well known
7. myself
8. sound of a clock
9. opposite of happy

Down

1. never making mistakes (para. 7)
2. international games (para. 4)
3. a kind of running and jumping race (para.4)
4. joined as husband and wife (para. 7)

Discovering

Find Out More

1. See if you can find a book about Babe Zaharias. Tell your friends the new things you learn about her.

2. Are there many girls in your school who like sports? They might like to hear about Babe. How do you feel about girls playing sports?

3. Are more women in sports now than in Babe's time? Name a few of today's women athletes and the sports they play.

4. Ask your teacher if you can have a classroom discussion on *The Way Women Are Treated in Sports.*

Captain Jones.

His own men wanted him to surrender. But this tough sea captain was ready to fight to the death.

The bullet had hit the sailor between the eyes. Blood spurted on the captain, who had been trying to help him. Smoke and noise made it hard to think. The ship was a wreck. Sails were torn with bullet holes. Some of the masts were broken. Many sailors were dead or wounded. The enemy ship was still firing all cannons. The captain knew his men wanted him to surrender. He knew he never would. I'll see us all dead first, he thought. *John Paul Jones* was not a quitter!

He was born in Scotland in 1747. His real name was John Paul. When he was twelve, he went to sea. He showed great talent as a sailor. When he was only twenty-two, he became captain of a ship. He was a tough skipper. Once, there was a mutiny on his ship. The sailors tried to take over. Captain John Paul killed one of the mutineers. When the ship returned to Scotland,

Daring Fighter

he was charged with murder. He knew he would not get a fair trial. One night he escaped from jail. He hid on a ship going to America.

When John Paul arrived in America he changed his name. He took the name John Paul Jones. In a few years, the Revolutionary War broke out. Jones now felt he was an American. He decided to fight against England. He was made a captain in the new United States Navy. He was given command of the *Ranger,* one of our first fighting ships.

Captain Jones was a daring fighter. He raided English ships at sea. He attacked seaports in England and Scotland. He also brought the United States one of its first sea victories. In a battle in the North Sea, he captured the *Drake,* an English warship. But in 1779, Jones won his greatest victory.

In September, Jones's ships met a large group of English ships. He was in command of the *Bonhomme Richard.* The *Bonhomme Richard* and the largest English ship, the *Serapis,* joined in battle. Jones's ship was much smaller. The large British ship had many more guns. Jones realized that there was only one way to win. He would have to get close and board the British ship. Jones used great skill to get close to the enemy ship. His ship was repeatedly hit by shells. Many people felt the American ship would sink. Once the English called for Jones to surrender. Jones gave his reply: "I have not yet begun to fight."

This reply gave his men new courage. The
two ships came together. The American gunners
shot the British sailors. After a fierce fight
with swords and handguns, the British
surrendered. The sea victory brought great pride
to America. Jones, a Scottish-American, became
a great hero of our country. It is no wonder he
is called "The Father of the American Navy."

Remembering

1. Which one of the following best states the *main idea* of paragraph 4? (Reread the paragraph.)
   a. Jones attacked seaports.
   b. Jones raided ships at sea.
   c. Jones was a daring fighter.
   d. Jones captured the *Drake.*

2. Which one or more of the following are *facts* presented in the story?
   a. John Paul was charged with murder.
   b. John almost drowned at sea.
   c. The *Drake* was an American ship.
   d. Jones fought in the Civil War.

3. Which one or more of the following are *facts* presented in the story?
   a. Jones won his greatest victory in 1779.
   b. Jones surrendered his ship to the English.
   c. Jones helped organize our army.
   d. John Paul killed a mutineer.

4. Even though *it doesn't say so* in the story, you can tell that:
   a. Jones was a sailor for twenty years before he became a sea captain.
   b. Many Americans thought Jones should return to Scotland.

c. Many sailors on the *Bonhomme Richard* were sharpshooters.

d. Jones battled in the Red Sea.

5. Which one of the following was mentioned *first* in the story?
   a. Jones escaped from jail.
   b. The *Serapis* was captured.
   c. Jones was twenty-two when he became a captain.
   d. English ships were raided.

6. The word *mutiny* (paragraph 2) means:
   a. a crash between two ships.
   b. a great fire at sea.
   c. a gang of crooks.
   d. a takeover of a ship by the crew.

7. The word *board* (paragraph 5) means:
   a. to go onto a ship.
   b. to make a large hole in a ship.
   c. a piece of lumber.
   d. to tow another ship.

8. A *poor* title for this story would be:
   a. The Great Sea Battle.
   b. The Victory of the *Serapis*.
   c. The Courageous Scotsman.
   d. Victory at Sea.

Discovering

Fun with Words: Analogies

Analogies are pairs of words that are related. It is fun to see words in pairs or in related ways. Look at the example. Then see if you can figure out the correct answers by using the words from the story. Work with a partner if you can. Here is an example:

Big is to *little* as *tall* is to:
a) round **b)** heavy **c)** short **d)** flat

The answer is *c, short*, because *little* is the opposite of *big* and *short* is the opposite of *tall.* Try the next few. If you need help, ask your teacher.

1. *Daring* (para. 4) is to *brave* as *fierce* (para. 6) is to:
   a) short **b)** slow **c)** weak **d)** violent

2. *Raided* (para. 4) is to *attacked* (para. 4) as *captured* (para. 4) is to:
   a) followed **b)** gave **c)** took **d)** repaired

3. *Victory* (para. 4) is to *failure* as *courage* (para. 6) is to:
   a) fear **b)** laughter **c)** bravery **d)** strength

4. *Skipper* (para. 2) is to *captain* (para. 2) as *command* (para. 3) is to:
   a) speed **b)** control **c)** payment **d)** beginning

Discovering

Find Out More

1. Go to the library and see if you can find a book or story about John Paul Jones. What other things can you learn about him? Discuss them with your classmates.

2. The American Navy has changed in many ways over the past 200 years. See what you can learn by making the following comparisons. Compare each item as it was during John Paul Jones's lifetime with how it is today.

   a. the amount of time it takes a ship to cross the Atlantic Ocean
   b. the kind of ships used by the Navy
   c. the instruments used by the Navy
   d. the number of men who work on a Navy ship
   e. what sailors' uniforms look like

3. Can you find out where John Paul Jones is buried? Ask your friends if they know. Don't tell the secret. Let them discover for themselves.

4. Would you like to build a model ship like the one John Paul Jones commanded? Ask your art teacher, woodshop teacher, or parents for ideas. Then go to it!

5. Do you know the different parts of a ship? Draw a picture of a ship and then label the parts.

Hero of the Opera House

Once he had to beg for a chance to sing.
Soon the whole world begged him to sing.

The lights grew dim and the crowd fell
silent. The curtain rose and the opera began.
Soon all eyes were on the star *Enrico Caruso.* His
powerful, yet rich and mellow, voice filled the
opera house. Time after time, his songs thrilled
the audience. When the final curtain came down,
the people went wild. They clapped till their
hands hurt. Each time Caruso came to take a
bow, they clapped harder. Soon they began to

chant, "Caruso! Caruso!" The great Caruso was
the most famous opera star alive. It is hard to
believe that this man's life had been filled with
sadness.

He was born in Italy. His parents were very
poor. When he was just a child, his mother
became very ill. Enrico left school and worked to
earn money to help his father support his family.
This did not seem to bother young Caruso. He

was always singing in his bright, mellow voice. Soon his singing became well known in the streets of Naples, Italy.

"If only you could have a teacher," people said. But young Caruso just smiled. "I need no teacher," he thought. "I can be a great singer on my own."

As Enrico grew, he had to work day and night. When no jobs were available, he would beg for money. He wanted to sing, but he could not find singing jobs. Soon he began begging for an opportunity to sing. One day a man from the Naples Opera Company heard Caruso singing in a cafe. He was amazed at the young tenor's power and range. He was told that Caruso's strong voice could break a glass. He asked Enrico to come and try out for a part in the opera. Caruso got the part and began his rise to fame and fortune.

Within a few years, the name Enrico Caruso was known all over the world. Many people believed his voice was one of the best ever heard. He sang in the world's greatest opera houses. People came by the thousands to hear him. He decided to go to America to sing at the Metropolitan Opera House. Here Enrico Caruso reached the height of his fame.

His popularity in America and Europe grew and grew. In the year of 1907-08, he earned more than a quarter of a million dollars. Most Americans knew the name Enrico Caruso. This great success and fame helped Italian-Americans. Many of them came to America as poor laborers.

They were looked down on and mistreated.
Caruso helped people realize that Italians had
great talent and skill. He helped Italians to become
accepted in America.

Few people realized Caruso was a sick
man. From early in his life, he suffered many
illnesses. He had severe headaches. He had
several operations on his throat to remove
growths. Because he sang with such force, he often
bled internally. But Caruso would not see a
doctor. He thought he could cure himself.

By 1920, Caruso was very ill. He continued
to sing, but he was always in great pain. After

each performance, he bled heavily. In December, 1920, he entered a hospital. His health continued to get worse. He died in July, 1921.

The whole world was saddened by his death. One of the greatest voices of all time was stilled. Yet Enrico Caruso left a mark on the world. All people, but especially Italian-Americans, took great pride in this genius. Today, the great Caruso has become a legend.

Remembering

1. Which one of the following best states the *main idea* of paragraph 7? (Reread the paragraph.)
   a. Caruso had severe headaches.
   b. Caruso had operations for growths.
   c. Caruso was a sick man.
   d. Caruso bled internally.

2. Which one or more of the following are *facts* presented in the story?
   a. Enrico was born in Italy.
   b. Caruso sang all over the world.
   c. Caruso never earned much money.
   d. Caruso's parents were wealthy.

3. Which one or more of the following are *facts* presented in the story?
   a. Caruso had two great teachers.
   b. Caruso sang at the Metropolitan Opera House.
   c. Caruso's voice was not too powerful.
   d. Italian-Americans disliked Caruso.

4. Even though *it doesn't say so* in the story, you can tell that:
   a. Caruso had great confidence in himself.
   b. Caruso became a star partly because people felt sorry for him.
   c. Caruso traveled all over the world to see different doctors.
   d. Most singers bleed internally.

Remembering

5. Which one of the following was mentioned *first* in in the story?
- **a.** Caruso begged for money.
- **b.** Caruso became very ill.
- **c.** Caruso came to America.
- **d.** Caruso sang in the Naples Opera Company.

6. The word *severe* (paragraph 7) means:
- **a.** serious.
- **b.** distracting.
- **c.** light.
- **d.** permanent.

7. The word *genius* (paragraph 9) means:
- **a.** a man.
- **b.** a teacher.
- **c.** a person with great talent.
- **d.** a rich person.

8. A *poor* title for this story would be:
- **a.** The Great Caruso.
- **b.** The Great Italian Glass Maker.
- **c.** From Beggar to Super Star.
- **d.** A Singing Legend.

Discovering

Fun with Words: Match Antonyms

Look at the words in Column A. See if you can figure out their *antonyms,* or opposite meanings, from the words in Column B. Match each word in Column A to its antonym in Column B. Write the words in your notebook. Look back in the story if you need to.

Column A

1. opportunity (para. 4)
2. mistreated (para. 6)
3. pride (para. 9)
4. realized (para. 7)

Column B

a. shame
b. taken care of
c. no chance
d. was unaware of

Find Out More

1. There are still old Caruso records available. See if you can locate one and listen to it. Why doesn't Caruso's voice sound more powerful on the record?

2. Try to find a picture of Enrico Caruso. Does he look like what you imagined? Write a brief paragraph telling your answer.

Vocabulary Review

STORIES 16-20

Following are some of the words you learned in the stories you have read. See if you can remember what these words mean. Try your hardest. Write your answers in your notebook.

1. *Monstrous* means:
   a) ugly. **b)** good looking. **c)** very big. **d)** beat up.

2. *Swarm* means:
   a) crowd around. **b)** question. **c)** make fun of. **d)** get an autograph.

3. *Executed* means:
   a) killed. **b)** sent out of the country. **c)** questioned. **d)** arrested.

4. *Scholar* means:
   a) an honest man. **b)** a very good student. **c)** a teacher. **d)** a listener.

5. *Amateur* means:
   a) a strong athlete. **b)** a beginner. **c)** a female athlete. **d)** a non-professional athlete.

6. *Instinct* means:
   a) having a good coach. **b)** showing great skill. **c)** deciding when to perform. **d)** natural ability.

7. *Mutiny* means:
   a) a crash. **b)** a fire. **c)** a crook. **d)** a takeover.

8. *Board* means:
   a) to go on. **b)** to drill a hole. **c)** to tow. **d)** to crash.

9. *Severe* means:
   a) serious. **b)** distracting. **c)** light. **d)** permanent.

10. *Genius* means:
    a) a man. **b)** a teacher. **c)** a rich person. **d)** a person with great talent.

Pioneer Poet

*She was only a baby when she was kidnapped
from Africa.
One day she would become America's first black poet.*

The ship sailed silently through the water.
It was dark in the tiny harbor off the coast of
West Africa. The only sound was the crying of a
five-year-old child. She was a kidnapped girl who
became known as *Lucy Terry.* She had been
taken from her parents. Now she was bound for
some unknown place. She never again saw
her home or loved ones. Like thousands of other
black Africans, she was sold as a slave.

Soon the slave ship arrived in America. Lucy was bought by a white man from Massachusetts. Her master proved to be a kind man. He taught her to read and write. Most slaves did not get the chance to learn reading and writing. Lucy learned to love books. She began to write stories. When her master died, Lucy was given her freedom.

In 1756, she was married to Abijah (ah BI juh) Prince, a free black. They then went to Northfield, Massachusetts, to work for the town minister. Abijah was a hard worker. As a reward, he was promised a 100-acre piece of land in the wilderness of what is now Vermont. After several years Lucy and Abijah decided to go to the new land.

In true pioneer spirit, they set out to establish their home. They worked hard and long to build their home. They cleared their land. They began raising their family of six children. While her husband worked in the fields, Lucy worked at home. At night, she wrote poetry and stories. Her stories and poems became well known. People came from far and wide to sit around the fireplace and hear "Luce" tell her tales. Her stories made their hard lives happier.

Life was not easy for the Princes. They had to fight the hardships of winter. They worked to clear their land of trees and brush. They struggled for a decent home like all other pioneers. Their sons joined the Green Mountain Boys and went to war. But the Princes had even another fight.

Because they were black, their white neighbors
frequently made trouble for them. Their neighbors
burned their hay, tore down their fences,
and even tried to take their land.

Eventually, the Princes sold their land and
bought more property in Southerland, Vermont.
They became founders of the territory. They
settled near the estate of Colonel Ethan Allen,
a famous Vermonter. They began the job of
building a home and clearing the land once more.

Almost immediately, they were told that
someone else claimed the land and was trying to
take it away. The case was brought all the
way up to the Federal Supreme Court. Lucy
argued her own case and she won. The Chief
Justice said Lucy's defense was the best one
he had ever heard. In fact, she won the case over
a Harvard graduate who later became the
Chief Justice of Vermont.

Years later this black woman gave a moving
speech to try to get her son into Williams
College in Massachusetts. But he was barred
because he was black.

Lucy Prince was not only one of the
earliest settlers of Vermont, but she was also
America's first black poet. The life of this pioneer
and writer is an inspiration to anyone facing
hardship and difficulty in their lives.

Remembering

1. Which one of the following best states the *main idea* of paragraph 4? (Reread the paragraph.)
   a. Lucy Terry sometimes wrote poetry and stories.
   b. Lucy worked in her home raising children.
   c. Lucy Terry and her husband were true pioneers.
   d. Mr. Prince worked to clear his land.

2. Which one or more of the following are *facts* presented in the story?
   a. Lucy lived in Vermont and Massachusetts.
   b. Lucy's son went to Williams College.
   c. Lucy and her husband never had problems with their neighbors.
   d. Lucy's sons joined the Green Mountain Boys.

3. Which one or more of the following are *facts* presented in the story?
   a. Lucy's husband was a free black.
   b. Lucy was kidnapped.
   c. It was not easy to clear land.
   d. Lucy learned to read and write.

4. Even though *it doesn't say so* in the story, you can tell that:
   a. Slavery existed in the North as well as the South.
   b. Lucy and her husband could not own land.
   c. Former slaves could not be heard in court.
   d. The Supreme Court was against Lucy.

165

5. Which one of the following was mentioned *first* in the story?
   a. Lucy and her husband tried to establish a home in the wilderness.
   b. Lucy lived in Northfield, Massachusetts.
   c. Lucy would entertain people with her stories and poems.
   d. Lucy's case went to the Supreme Court.

6. The word *kidnapped* (paragraph 1) means:
   a. killed.
   b. borrowed.
   c. taken illegally.
   d. saved.

7. The word *moving* (paragraph 8) means:
   a. continuing.
   b. going from one place to another.
   c. causing people to feel you are right.
   d. causing great anger.

8. A *poor* title for this story would be:
   a. The Story of a Kidnapped Girl.
   b. The Woman Lawyer.
   c. An Early Black Pioneer.
   d. A Great Black Woman.

Discovering

Fun with Words: Synonyms

Words often have many meanings. Words that mean the same thing, or almost the same thing, are called *synonyms.* Below are several words that mean the same thing as a word used in the story. Look at the words and see if you can find the word in the story that has the same meaning.

1. honorable, respectable, appropriate, worthy: (para. 5)

2. motivation, spirit, drive, encouragement: (para. 9)

3. property, homestead, land holdings, grounds: (para. 6)

4. denied, refused, banned, not permitted: (para. 8)

5. resistance, protection, stand, safeguard: (para. 7)

Find Out More

1. The Green Mountain Boys were mentioned in the story. Can you find out any more about them and what they did? We will give you a hint by telling you they were involved in the American Revolution.

2. Locate on a map the places where Lucy lived in New England.

3. There are many black poets. See if you can find some of their poetry in your library.

4. Have you ever tried to write a poem? Write one about an adventure that you had. Share your poem with your classmates.

Musical Ambassador

As a boy he disliked classical music.
As a man he became the world's greatest violinist.

Everyone held their breath with fear. What Jewish family was being taken away by the secret police? What had they done? Why were they being sent away from their home? The screams and cries of the little children were silenced by the shouting police. Soon the night became quiet again. All the Jews living in the Jewish ghetto were fearful. Who would be next?

Some of these Russian Jews had heard of America. Perhaps, there a Jew did not live in fear.

Mr. Stern decided that he, his wife, and baby
son Isaac would leave Russia. They would seek
a new life in America. He sold everything they
had to get the money for the boat fare. One cold
day, the family left Russia for America.

Life in America was not easy. The Sterns had
to work hard to earn a living. Some people were
not nice to Jews. But at least the Sterns did
not live in fear.

Mrs. Stern loved music. She had taught

piano in Russia. She loved to play and often entertained her family and friends. It was natural for young *Isaac Stern* to begin to enjoy music. At the age of six he started piano lessons. He was taken to many classical concerts. His life was full of music.

At first, Isaac did not always enjoy the lessons and concerts. He would rather play with his friends. A career in music was not for him. Then Isaac discovered the violin. He wanted to learn to play it, but his parents were too poor to pay for lessons. He tried to learn on his own, but progress was slow.

When he was ten, some wealthy women heard him play. They felt this boy had great talent. They offered to pay for Isaac's lessons. He was sent to the San Francisco Conservatory of Music. He immediately showed signs of unusual talent for the violin. He also showed himself to be a dedicated student. He often practiced eight hours a day.

One year later, at the age of eleven, he played with the San Francisco Symphony. Six years later, he appeared as a soloist in New York City. The critics were not very impressed. Isaac decided to really prove himself. He returned to San Francisco. For the next several years, he studied even harder. During these years, he played in many concerts. Finally, he felt he was ready.

He returned to New York City to play at Carnegie Hall. This was quite a thrill for a young man of twenty-one. Everyone wondered whether

he was really ready. Isaac's playing was beautiful. The critics said he played better than all other American violinists. Isaac Stern became famous overnight.

Over the years, he played in almost every country in the world. He gave many concerts to raise money to help Jews and other people in need. He worked with the United States government to encourage music students. He spent time entertaining American soldiers overseas. Isaac also performed in films, on radio, and on television. You may not think you have heard him, but maybe you have. If you saw the movie *Fiddler on the Roof,* it was Isaac Stern's violin playing you heard during the movie.

Isaac Stern is a musical ambassador. He has used his music to bring people together. He has helped people to better understand each other. He is a source of pride not only to Jewish-Americans, but to all Americans.

Remembering

1. Which one of the following best states the *main idea* of paragraph 8? (Reread the paragraph.)
   a. Isaac played in Carnegie Hall.
   b. People were waiting for Isaac's return.
   c. Stern's playing was beautiful.
   d. Stern became a star overnight.

2. Which one or more of the following are *facts* presented in the story?
   a. Isaac was born in Russia.
   b. Isaac attended many concerts.
   c. Isaac enjoyed playing the piano.
   d. The violin was the first instrument Isaac learned to play.

3. Which one or more of the following are *facts* presented in the story?
   a. Isaac studied at the Los Angeles Conservatory.
   b. Isaac's parents were wealthy people.
   c. Isaac performed all over the world.
   d. Isaac lived in San Francisco.

4. Even though *it doesn't say so* in the story, you can tell that:
   a. Isaac's parents did not think he could earn much money as a musician.
   b. The Sterns were a rich family.

    c. Even talented musicians must practice many hours.

    d. Isaac was ashamed of being a Jew.

5. Which one of the following was mentioned *first* in the story?
    a. Isaac began playing the piano.
    b. The Sterns left Russia.
    c. Isaac attended the Conservatory.
    d. Isaac played in concerts all over the world.

6. The word *classical* (paragraph 4) means:
    a. rhythm and blues music.
    b. rock and roll music.
    c. music from Broadway shows.
    d. a kind of serious music, like operas.

7. The word *ambassador* (paragraph 10) means:
    a. a performer of the arts.
    b. a coach of music.
    c. a teacher of music.
    d. a person who helps people to understand each other.

8. A *poor* title for this story would be:
    a. The Great Violinist.
    b. The Inventor of the Violin.
    c. The Musical Ambassador.
    d. A Musical Genius.

Discovering

Fun with Words: Crossword Puzzle

Copy the crossword puzzle into your notebook. Then fill in the white boxes with the correct words.

Across

5. a musical instrument (para. 5)
6. to study and remember (para. 5)
7. opposite of he (para. 4)
8. opposite of night (para. 2)
10. assist; give aid (para. 9)

Down

1. in faraway places (para. 9)
2. musical shows (para. 4)
3. poor—two words (para. 9)
4. a feeling of being afraid (para. 2)
9. how old something is (para. 7)

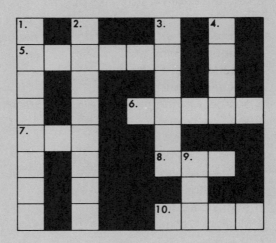

Discovering

Find Out More

1. The violin is an interesting instrument. See if you can find out how it was invented. How does music come from a violin? One person you can get information about music from is your music teacher.

2. See if anyone in the class or your teacher has the record "Fiddler on the Roof." Listen to the violin playing of Isaac Stern. How do you feel when you hear his music? Do you enjoy it more because you know something about him? Discuss your answers with your teacher and classmates.

A BLOCK OF GRANITE

*His coach thought Vince was too little to play football.
But one day he was to become "Mr. Football."*

The crowd roared as the kickoff sailed down
the field. The receiver took it and dashed across
the field. He cut back toward the middle and
was snowed under by tacklers. As the Fordham
team went to the huddle, they were confident.
"O.K., Lombardi and you other guys, open those
holes," said the quarterback.

On the next play, the charging Fordham
linemen ripped huge holes in the defense. The
play went for big yardage. Again and again the
line opened huge holes. Thanks to the line, the

team scored many touchdowns. Within a few years, this group of linemen became a legend. They came to be known as the "seven blocks of granite." Just like granite rock, they were tough. They went down in history as one of the greatest lines in college history. One of these linemen was a man named *Vince Lombardi.*

Vince was much smaller than any of the other linemen. At first his coaches thought he was too small to play. But Vince was determined to make up for his size with effort and hard work. He just kept thinking, "I can do it." And he did it. He and the other "blocks of granite" helped Fordham win most of their games.

When Lombardi graduated from college, he decided to teach. He taught chemistry, physics, and algebra. He also became the football coach at St. Cecelia's High School in Englewood, New Jersey. Anyone that played for him had to be dedicated. Football was not a game. It was a way of life. On the field, Lombardi made sure his players were tough. Off the field, his players were gentlemen. He was both coach and leader.

His teams were unbeatable. Soon colleges wanted him to coach their teams. Lombardi went to West Point as line coach. This was proof of his success. Coaching at a military academy was something! During his six years there, his teams again were winners.

Professional football coaching seemed an impossible dream for Lombardi. But he was asked to become an assistant coach for the New York Giants. Lombardi knew this was a tough

assignment. But his dedication and love of
the game were always there. The Giants proved
to be a winner with Lombardi.

At this time, there was a team called the
Green Bay Packers. This professional team
came from a very small city in Wisconsin. The
team lost almost every game it played. Fans from
big cities laughed at them. Green Bay was a real
loser. They needed a great coach and leader.

In 1959, Vince Lombardi was asked to come
to Green Bay. Going from New York to Green
Bay was a great change. But Lombardi was
determined to build a winner. The job would
not be easy.

Lombardi brought spirit and confidence to the

team. Men who played for him felt his power and dedication. They somehow felt stronger, more confident. Each man felt like winning.

He was a tough, demanding coach. He expected his players to be in shape. He expected them to always give 100 per cent. Each play had to run perfectly. Training rules were never broken. Any man who disobeyed him was out. As a result, players both loved and hated Coach Lombardi.

All this work and dedication soon paid off. Lombardi worked with the Green Bay Packers for nine seasons. His team won five NFL Championships. They also won the first two superbowls. Many experts feel his team was the greatest ever. Lombardi was recognized as a "super coach."

He decided to take on another challenge. The Washington Redskins were also losers. They did not have a winning season for 14 years. Lombardi was asked to become coach, general manager, and part owner. The first year he was there the Redskins had a winning season. Lombardi *was* a miracle worker!

One day, Vince became ill. He had cancer. In just a few months, Vince Lombardi was dead. Fans and players all mourned his death. This Italian-American was truly loved by all Americans. His determination and spirit will always be remembered in sports.

Remembering

1. Which one of the following best states the *main idea of* paragraph 10? (Reread the paragraph.)
   a. All players had to be in shape.
   b. Lombardi was a demanding coach.
   c. Each play had to be run perfectly.
   d. Lombardi expected training rules to be followed.

2. Which one or more of the following are *facts* presented in the story?
   a. The Washington Redskins had 14 winning seasons.
   b. Lombardi taught chemistry.
   c. Green Bay is a large city in Wisconsin.
   d. Lombardi once coached the New York Giants.

3. Which one or more of the following are *facts* presented in the story?
   a. Lombardi was also a great hockey coach.
   b. Vince was a great football player.
   c. Lombardi coached at Annapolis Military Academy.
   d. Green Bay won five NFL Championships.

4. Even though *it doesn't say so* in the story, you can tell that:
   a. A coach is an important part of a team.
   b. All of the men known as the "seven blocks of granite" became coaches.

181

   c. Only big cities can have good football teams.

   d. When Lombardi left Green Bay, many of the Packers joined the Washington Redskins.

5. Which one of the following was mentioned *first* in the story?

   a. Lombardi coached at West Point.

   b. Lombardi became part owner of the Redskins.

   c. Vince was one of the "blocks of granite."

   d. Lombardi went to the Packers.

6. The word *granite* (paragraph 2) means:

   a. a good team.

   b. a hard person.

   c. a kind of stone.

   d. a kind of metal.

7. The word *dedicated* (paragraph 4) means:

   a. good looking.

   b. easy going.

   c. hard working.

   d. interesting.

8. A *poor* title for this story would be:

   a. The Green Bay Packers.

   b. A Winning Coach.

   c. A Dedicated Football Coach.

   d. The Man Who Became a Football Legend.

Discovering

Fun with Words: Scramble

Below are some of the words from the story. They are scrambled, or all mixed up. See if you can figure out what each word is. Write the words in your notebook. You can look back at the story for clues. Try your hardest!

1. ncfdncoiee (para. 9)
2. dmndngeai (para. 10)
3. cmhstreiy (para. 4)
4. bntblueaae (para. 5)
5. lnssfproeioa (para. 6)

Find Out More

1. Football is a popular game in America. In which other countries do people play football?

2. How many professional football teams are there in this country? How many leagues are there? Does a team play another team more than once in the same year?

3. If you would like to read more about Vince Lombardi, check your school library. If you can't find a book about him, ask your librarian to help you.

4. A trophy is named after Vince Lombardi. Can you find out which one it is? See if your friends know what the trophy is called. Don't tell them! Let them find out for themselves.

BLOOD

DOCTOR

*There was no American school or college
that would take this man.*

"Look out," screamed the woman. It was too
late. The two cars smashed head on. Glass
and metal tore the bodies of the drivers and
passengers. By the time help arrived, all the
injured had lost much blood. They could be
saved only by a blood transfusion (tranz FEW
zhun). A transfusion means giving a hurt person
blood that has been stored away. The transfusion
was given and the injured people's lives were
saved!

If no one had discovered how to store blood,
millions of people would die. The person who
discovered how to store blood deserves many
thanks. Who was this person?

Charles Drew had just graduated from high
school. He was an outstanding student and an
all-around athlete. His one dream was to
become a doctor, but getting into medical college

was not easy. It was even harder for a black man. One American school after another turned Drew down. Each time a different reason was given but the answer was always "no." He decided that, if American schools did not want blacks, he would study in another country. He went to a medical school in Canada.

He studied for many years at McGill Medical School in Montreal, Canada. Drew saw many injured and sick people die from loss of blood. Day and night, he thought about this problem. He did experiments. Sometimes he worked all day and all night, trying to discover the mystery of blood. He thought blood could be given by one person to another. Blood could be stored, but it changed during storage. Drew wondered how this change could be stopped.

One day, Drew discovered how to remove the cells from blood and to preserve the whole blood that was left. This was the discovery of blood plasma, one of the greatest medical discoveries of all time. Millions of people could now be saved. Wounded soldiers, sick people, and people injured in accidents could be saved because of Dr. Drew's work.

Now that he was famous, America recognized the doctor who earlier was turned away from American medical schools. During World War I, Drew was asked to become Medical Director of the Red Cross in Europe. He helped set up the blood bank that provided the blood which saved many lives.

Dr. Drew was now famous and recognized as
a great medical scientist. However, he was still
troubled by the racial problem in America. Blacks
could neither give blood nor receive white blood.
Many doctors refused to accept blood donations
from anyone but whites. Even when Dr. Drew
proved *all* blood was basically the same, the
situation did not change. Dr. Drew resigned from
the Red Cross. In this way, he drew attention
to the discrimination against black Americans.

Dr. Drew was given many honors and
degrees by universities in America. He was still
unhappy because of the treatment his people

received, and he continued to speak out for blacks. One day at the age of 46, Dr. Drew was seriously injured in an auto accident. A hospital for whites was nearby, but he had to be taken a long distance to a black hospital. During the long trip, he died from loss of blood. Dr. Drew, who had done so much to save millions of lives, died because he could not receive blood at a white hospital. Only in recent years have Americans come to fully appreciate this great man's work. Dr. Drew was truly "the Blood Maker" and the giver of life.

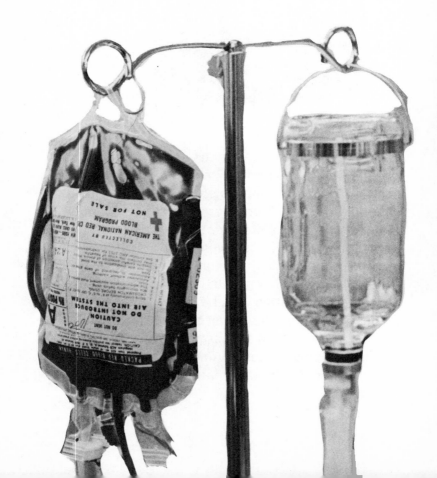

Remembering

1. Which one of the following best states the *main idea of* paragraph 4? (Reread the paragraph.)
   a. Drew discovered blood plasma.
   b. Cells could be removed from blood.
   c. Many lives could be saved.
   d. Drew worked hard.

2. Which one or more of the following are *facts* presented in the story?
   a. Dr. Drew could not get accepted by a medical school in America.
   b. Dr. Drew was shot.
   c. Dr. Drew was an excellent athlete.
   d. Dr. Drew discovered how to store blood for long periods of time.

3. Which one or more of the following are *facts* presented in the story?
   a. Dr. Drew studied at McGill University.
   b. Dr. Drew worked for the Red Cross.
   c. Dr. Drew discovered heart surgery.
   d. Dr. Drew did few experiments on blood.

4. Even though *it doesn't say so* in the story, you can tell that: (Mark one.)
   a. Canada did not have serious racial problems.
   b. Dr. Drew was easily discouraged.
   c. Blood transfusions were easy to discover.
   d. The Red Cross was founded by a black man.

Remembering

5. Which of the following was mentioned *first* in the story?
   a. Dr. Drew resigned from the European Red Cross.
   b. Dr. Drew was denied acceptance to medical schools in America.
   c. Dr. Drew discovered how to store blood.
   d. Dr. Drew founded the blood bank system.

6. The word *discrimination* (paragraph 7) means:
   a. not realizing something.
   b. not sharing.
   c. not treating someone equally.
   d. trying to destroy someone.

7. The word *wounded* (paragraph 5) means:
   a. injured.   c. destroyed.
   b. killed.   d. captured.

8. A *poor* title for this story would be:
   a. A Great Scientist.
   b. The Discovery of Blood Plasma.
   c. A Famous Doctor.
   d. Diseases of the Blood.

Discovering

Fun with Words: Analogies

Analogies are pairs of words that are related. It is fun to see words in pairs or in related ways. Look at the example. Then see if you can figure out the correct answers by using the words from the story.

Big is to *little* as *tall* is to:
a) round   **b)** heavy   **c)** short   **d)** flat

The answer is *(c), short,* because *little* is the opposite of *big* and *short* is the opposite of *tall.*

1. *Discovered* (para. 2) is to *found* as *resigned* (para. 7) is to:
   a) joined   **b)** released   **c)** lost   **d)** quit
2. *Provided* (para. 6) is to *supplied* as *preserve* (para. 5) is to:
   a) destroy   **b)** spend   **c)** keep   **d)** purchase
3. *Automobiles* is to *cars* as *donations* (para. 7) is to:
   a) floods   **b)** gifts   **c)** payments   **d)** persons
4. *Famous* (para. 6) is to *unknown* as *troubled* (para. 7) is to:
   a) content   **b)** upset   **c)** unhappy   **d)** tired

Find Out More

Although all blood is *basically* the same, it does differ in *type.*
   a. How many different types of blood are there?
   b. Which type is most common?
   c. Which type is most rare?

Vocabulary Review

STORIES 21-24

Following are some of the words you learned in the stories you have read. See if you can remember what these words mean. Try your hardest. Write your answers in your notebook.

1. *Kidnapped* means:
   a) saved. **b)** taken illegally. **c)** borrowed.
   d) killed.

2. *Moving* means:
   a) causing anger. **b)** causing people to feel you are right. **c)** unhappy. **d)** continuing.

3. *Classical* means:
   a) rhythm and blues music. **b)** rock and roll music.
   c) music from Broadway shows. **d)** serious music, like opera.

4. *Ambassador* means:
   a) a performer. **b)** a coach. **c)** a teacher. **d)** a goodwill representative.

5. *Granite* means:
   a) a team. **b)** a hard person. **c)** a stone. **d)** a metal.

6. *Dedicated* means:
   a) good looking. **b)** easy going. **c)** hard working. **d)** interesting.

7. *Discrimination* means:
   a) not realizing something. **b)** trying to destroy someone. **c)** not sharing. **d)** not treating someone equally.

8. *Wounded* means:
   a) destroyed. **b)** captured. **c)** injured. **d)** killed.

Vocabulary Review

STORIES 1-24

Following are some of the words you learned in the stories you have read. See if you can remember what these words mean. Try your hardest. Write your answers in your notebook.

1. *Disaster* means:
   a) a serious crime.   **b)** a joke.   **c)** something that causes loss of life or property.   **d)** an unusual discovery.

2. *Illustrating* means:
   a) writing.   **b)** printing.   **c)** drawing.   **d)** selling.

3. *Discrimination* means:
   a) trying to destroy someone.   **b)** not sharing.   **c)** not treating someone equally.   **d)** not realizing something.

4. *Instinct* means:
   a) having a good coach.   **b)** showing great skill.   **c)** deciding when to perform.   **d)** natural ability.

194

5. *Wastelands* means:
a) small pieces of land. **b)** land where many people live. **c)** deserts. **d)** places not fit for human life.

6. *Professional* means:
a) playing for money. **b)** a man who changes the rules. **c)** playing in tournaments. **d)** playing for the fun of it.

7. *Adopted* means:
a) purchased. **b)** destroyed. **c)** denied. **d)** took as your own.

8. *Dominated* means:
a) discussed. **b)** trained. **c)** gave. **d)** controlled.

9. *Accomplishments* means:
a) fears. **b)** understandings. **c)** things that have been done well. **d)** partners.

10. *Trampled* means:
a) bumped. **b)** afraid. **c)** crushed. **d)** pushed.

11. *Founded* means:
    a) discovered. **b)** started. **c)** enlarged. **d)** pur-
    chased.

12. *Denied* means:
    a) refused. **b)** accepted. **c)** permitted. **d)** rec-
    ognized.

13. *Severe* means:
    a) serious. **b)** distracting. **c)** light. **d)** perma-
    nent.

14. *Powerhouse* means:
    a) someone who is very handsome. **b)** someone
    who is wealthy. **c)** something that is very strong.
    d) a storeroom.

15. *Genius* means:
    a) a man. **b)** a teacher. **c)** a rich person. **d)** a
    person with great talent.

16. *Amateur* means:
    a) a non-professional athlete. **b)** a beginner.
    c) a female athlete. **d)** a strong athlete.

17. *Granite* means:
  a) a team. **b)** a hard person. **c)** a stone. **d)** a metal.

18. *Inspiration* means:
  a) a show-off. **b)** someone who makes you worry.
  c) something that makes you try. **d)** a poor example.

19. *Classical* means:
  a) rhythm and blues music. **b)** rock and roll music. **c)** music from Broadway shows. **d)** serious music, like opera.

20. *Handicapped* means:
  a) having an unusual problem. **b)** unusually strong. **c)** without great talent. **d)** not living in a big city.

21. *Horror* means:
  a) scary. **b)** entertaining. **c)** shown at midnight.
  d) easy to make.

22. *Suspended* means:
    a) taken away. **b)** changed. **c)** enforced.
    d) voted for by the people.

23. *Trademark* means:
    a) a name. **b)** a kind of title. **c)** the way people
    or things are recognized. **d)** a discovery.

24. *Wealthy* means:
    a) old. **b)** rich. **c)** well educated. **d)** talented.

25. *Scarce* means:
    a) difficult. **b)** unimportant. **c)** hard to get.
    d) not paying much.

Reading
First Aid

A Cure for
Those Who Miss Main Ideas

A well-written paragraph (a group of related sentences) always has a *main idea.* The main idea tells you what the whole paragraph is about. Let's look at an example.

Example One

The leopard is an amazing animal. He is very strong and very fast. One blow from his paw can kill a man. He has been clocked at 60 m.p.h. He is one of the smartest hunters in the jungle. He plans each kill and then waits for his victim.

Which sentence tells us what the whole paragraph is about? "The leopard is an amazing animal." Why is this answer right? The paragraph makes the following statements about the leopard: *He is strong. He is fast. He is smart.* These sentences explain why the leopard is an amazing animal. So you can see that the whole paragraph is about the leopard, an amazing animal. That is why this is the main idea of the paragraph.

Let's see if you understand. Try another example.

Example Two

A smart shopper must always be alert. Some packages cheat the buyer. They look big, but they may contain less than a smaller box. Some stores try to get people to buy things they don't need. Many items are placed near the check-out lines. This may make you buy them even though you don't need them.

Did you figure out the sentence that gave the main idea? The main idea is: "A smart shopper must always be alert." Why is this answer right? The paragraph tells us the following reasons why a shopper must be alert: *Some packages cheat the buyer. Some stores try to get you to buy things you don't need.* The whole paragraph is about smart shoppers and why they must be alert.

Here are some paragraphs you can try on your own. Read the paragraphs carefully. Try to pick out the main idea. Then try to find the reasons why it is the main idea. Put your answers in your notebook. Be alert.

1.

Isaac Hayes is truly an exciting performer. His music is original and rhythmic. His costumes are very mod and different. He sings in a low, mellow voice. The songs that he chooses tell the story of the black man's experience.

2.

Going to Montreal, Canada, is like going to France. You hear people speaking French wherever you go. You see many cafés, or small restaurants, as in French towns. The buildings are very similar to those you would see in a French city. The style of dress is almost exactly the same as in Paris.

3.

Why are so many people going camping today? This activity enables people to get outdoors and enjoy nature. Compared to motels and hotels, camping costs very little. It is an excellent family activity that all can enjoy. The camper has an opportunity to enjoy the birds, animals, and the forest.

4.

More and more people have begun to ride bicycles. This sport is excellent exercise for everyone. Once you buy your bike, bicycling costs very little. Some real bike fans enjoy racing. Many people use bikes for transportation. But probably the most important reason that people ride bikes is that it is fun.

Tennis has an interesting history. It started out as a game played by kings and queens. It was called the "royalty game." Large tennis courts were built in castles. Instead of a net, a large mound of dirt was used. Later the courts were moved outside. This is when the game became known as "lawn tennis." Today it is usually called just "tennis."

In all of these examples, the main idea is the first sentence. This is sometimes called the *topic sentence*. Sometimes there is no topic sentence. You must read the whole paragraph. Then you decide what the main idea is. Let's look at an example.

Example One

On the way to school this morning, I saw two squirrels chasing each other. I later saw two dogs wrestling. When I got to school, two chipmunks were playing tag in the grass. It did not surprise me when I saw two kittens jumping over the fence.

What is the main idea of this paragraph? The main idea is: *I saw animals playing this morning on the way to school.* Why is this the main idea? The entire paragraph tells you about what I saw this morning on my way to school.

See if you can figure out the main idea of each of the following paragraphs. Be alert. Don't get fooled. Put your answers in your notebook.

1.

First the tin cans are placed on a belt. As the cans pass through the machine, they are painted. Each can is then boiled. Farther along, the can is filled and sealed. Finally, the can is packed in a crate and stored.

2.

The sea contains many minerals and chemicals. It is the source of much of our food. It also provides a way of transportation. Many people use the sea for recreation and sport. Practically everyone loves the sea.

3.

Tobacco was first discovered by the Indians. They thought it had some medical power. They smoked it and used it in medicines. Early explorers brought it back to Europe. It soon became fashionable to smoke. At that time, few people realized the danger of smoking.

4.

At first I thought flying was hard. I looked at all the dials and got scared. I later began to realize that only a few instruments are really important. The rudder, the stick, the throttle, and the altimeter are really the most important ones. But I always check all the others, too.

5.

Riding a horse begins with getting used to the horse. Pat him and talk to him. Try to be relaxed. When you mount, always use the left side. Get a firm grip on the reins with your left hand. Place your left foot in the stirrup. Hold the saddle with both hands. Now pull yourself up and on.

A Cure for
Those Who Miss Supporting Details

A well-written paragraph (a group of related sentences) has a main idea. This main idea tells what the whole paragraph is about. A well-written paragraph also has sentences that give information about the main idea in the paragraph. These sentences are called *supporting details.* These details help make the paragraph clear. They also give the reader important information. A good reader must learn how to recognize these details. He must also learn how to remember them. Let's see if you understand what supporting details are. Look at the following example.

Oil is one of man's most useful resources. It is used for fuel for homes. It is needed to make medicines. The plastic industry could not function without it. Rubber products use oil as a basic material. Oil is also the source of gasoline for cars and airplanes.

The main idea is: *Oil is one of man's most useful resources.* What are the supporting details that tell us about the main idea? Can you find them? Look back and try.

The supporting details are as follows:

1. It is used for fuel for homes.

2. It is needed to make medicines.

3. The plastic industry could not function without it.

4. Rubber products use oil as a basic material.

5. Oil is the source of gasoline.

These sentences are supporting details in the paragraph. They help us see why the main idea is true.

Let's see if you understand. Try finding the main idea and supporting details in the following paragraph.

Example Two

South Africa is a nation that treats many of its citizens unfairly. Black citizens are victims of racial discrimination. They are not allowed decent jobs. They must live in special housing. They cannot participate in government. Black universities are not allowed. Many citizens have been denied the protection of the law.

Did you locate the main idea and supporting details?

The main idea is: *South Africa is a nation that treats many of its citizens unfairly.*

The supporting details are:

1. Black citizens are victims of racial discrimination.

2. They don't have decent jobs.

3. They must live in special housing.

4. They cannot participate in government.

5. Black universities are not allowed.

6. Black citizens have been denied the protection of the law.

In the exercises found in this book you are asked to identify details found in the stories. If you learn to be alert for details when reading, you can do this type of question easily. Following are some paragraphs to work on. Read the paragraphs carefully. Try to remember the supporting details as you read them. Then, without looking back, see if you can answer the questions. Be on the alert. Don't get fooled. Put your answers in your notebook.

1.

Many different kinds of exercise help keep your body in shape. Toe touching helps keep the stomach flat. Jumping jacks help circulation. Push-ups strengthen the arms, shoulders, and chest. Chin-ups or sit-ups are great for the back muscles.

Which one or more of the following are *facts* presented in the paragraph?
a. Jumping jacks keep the stomach flat.
b. Chin-ups and sit-ups help the back muscles.
c. Toe touching keeps the stomach flat.
d. Exercise keeps your body in shape.

2.

Some television stars get thousands of dollars for a few minutes work. There are people who get a lot of money just to answer a question. Millions of dollars are earned by people who never work a day. They let their money work for them. Sometimes the amount of work people do has nothing to do with how much money they make.

Which one or more of the following are *facts* presented in the paragraph?
a. You don't make money if you don't work long hours.

b. Some people make millions of dollars but don't work.

c. Television stars get thousands of dollars for a few minutes work.

d. No one is paid a lot of money to give an opinion.

Here are some longer reading selections. Remember to be alert for details. Read the following and answer the questions that follow.

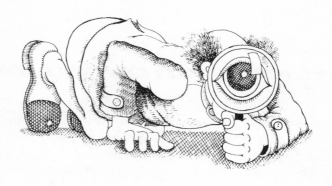

3.

Many students depend on scholarships to go to college. Some students receive awards based on their good grades earned in high school. Those with athletic ability receive athletic scholarships to cover expenses. Students with talent in music and art often receive aid because of their ability in these fields.

Of all these scholarships, the one given for athletics is probably the most demanding. In order to continue on scholarship, performance is necessary. Long, hard practice sessions become a way of life. Even after the season for the sport is over, practice continues. In addition, school work must remain satisfactory. If grades go down, the scholarship is lost. College athletes have a tough life.

Which one or more of the following are *facts* presented in the story?
a. Athletic scholarships are most demanding.
b. Scholarships are easy to get.
c. No scholarships are given to students with high grades.
d. Practice continues year round for students on an athletic scholarship.

4.

Track and field events require great physical ability. Many require physical strength. Others require speed and endurance. All the events require practice, training, and discipline.

The events that require the greatest physical strength are the javelin throw, shot-put, pole-vault, hammer-throw, and the discus.

Endurance and speed are essential for the long jump, dashes, and long-distance running. An athlete unwilling to discipline his mind and body will never make it in track and field.

Disciplining mind and body sounds easy. It's not. Everyone enjoys parties, fattening foods, and late hours. Some people like smoking and drinking. Athletes like many of these things. But if they hope to be champions in track and field, they must give up many of these things. In addition, maintaining top physical shape requires hours of practice. This may mean giving up hobbies and other things that are fun to do. All of this means discipline. No, it's not easy!

1. Which one or more of the following are *facts* presented in the story?
   a. Some events require great physical strength.
   b. Pole-vaulting requires speed.
   c. Discipline is easy.
   d. Hammer-throws require speed.

2. Which one or more of the following are *facts* presented in the story?
   a. Long-distance running requires endurance.
   b. Winning takes mental discipline.
   c. Athletes do not like parties.
   d. Sacrifices are necessary to be a champion.

A Cure for
Those Who Miss Inferences

Inference questions are probably the hardest
kind to answer. In main idea questions, you can
read the paragraph and find the answer. In detail
questions, the answers are also right in the paragraph. But in inference questions, the answer is
not in the paragraph. You must first read the paragraph. You put together all the information in the
paragraph. You then use this information to make
an inference. Even though it is not written, you
can figure out what the inference is. Look at the
example to see what we mean.

Example One

John used to come over and play. Every time John came, my mother found money missing. Now John can't come and play. We no longer find money missing.

Even though *it doesn't say it,* what does the paragraph seem to tell us about John? *John steals.* Do you see why? The passage doesn't come right out and say John steals. But if you put together all the information, you can tell that he does.

Try the next example.

Example Two

In India elephants are used like trucks. They move huge trees and logs. They push giant rocks. Sometimes they are hitched to wagons and pull heavy loads of dirt.

Even though *it doesn't say it*, what does the paragraph seem to tell us about elephants? *Elephants are very strong.* Do you see why? The paragraph tells us that elephants do lots of work. It also tells us they do heavy work. In order for them to do this, they must be very strong. You know this, even though it doesn't say it in the paragraph.

Now try a longer paragraph. Read carefully and think.

Example Three

Most movie stars get up around 5 A.M. They report to the studio for makeup by 7. They spend about nine hours under hot lights. Sometimes a scene must be filmed ten or eleven times. If the movie is being filmed outdoors, a change in weather could force the scene to be done all over. Meals are usually sandwiches and coffee. Lunch times are only 15 or 20 minutes long.

Even though *it doesn't say so* in the paragraph, you can tell that:
- **a.** Movie stars earn a lot of money.
- **b.** Actors get a lot of time for meals.
- **c.** Acting in movies is hard work.
- **d.** Weather changes do not affect filming.

217

If you chose *a*, *b*, or *d*, you picked the wrong answer. The paragraph says nothing about how much money actors earn. It says meals are only 15 or 20 minutes, which is not much time at all. Weather changes can mean that a scene must be done over. So they surely must affect filming. The correct answer is *c*. If you put all the information together, you can figure out that acting is hard work.

Now try making some inferences on your own. Read carefully and think.

The crowd roars. The home team charges onto the field. Their uniforms are bright in the afternoon sun. The band is playing. Cheerleaders are going through their acts. Coaches and assistants are busy on the sidelines. The crowd is quickly filling the stands. It's Saturday, and it is nearly kickoff time.

All during the week, the team has been working. They have had daily practice. Players have hit each other. Some have been injured. Kickers have made hundreds of kicks. Plays have been run over and over again. Coaches have spent many hours drilling the team. Trainers have fixed many cuts and sprains.

The band has also practiced all week. They have spent many hours playing music. They have spent more hours on field formations. Twirlers and flag carriers have been busy working on their jobs. The cheerleaders have tried many new moves. They have developed some new stunts. Now everything is ready.

Even though *it doesn't say so* in the story, you can tell that:

    a. The actual game is only a small part of the work involved.

    b. Practice sessions were held twice.

    c. The band is larger than most.

    d. Cheerleaders do not work on their stunts.

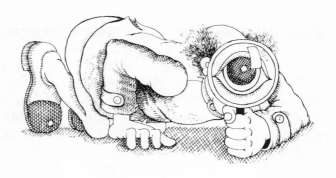

2.

Flying off to strange new places is exciting. Meeting different people and seeing new sights is fun. Wearing a colorful uniform is fun, too. No wonder so many men and women want to be airline stewards and stewardesses. First, they must send in an application. If they are lucky, they are accepted for training. Before long, they will be flying.

Training begins with many hours of classroom work. Hours are spent on personal grooming. Lessons are even given in speech training.

Next the trainees are given courses in first aid. They are also taught what to do in case of crash landings. They are given instructions on lifesaving and the use of safety equipment.

Learning how to handle trays and food comes next. Stewards and stewardesses must know how to do this even in rough weather.

Mixing drinks and pouring and serving hot liquids are included in the training program.

Now comes the actual flight practice. The trainees are taken up in planes. They practice all the things they have learned. Some of them find the job is harder when the plane is in the air. If they pass flight practice, they are ready to fly as junior stewards and stewardesses.

Junior stewards and stewardesses work with a more experienced person. This person helps them learn about the job. They meet passengers and begin to find out what the job is really like.

Once they become full stewards and stewardesses, they must work very hard. Making passengers comfortable, serving meals and drinks, and doing lots of other things can make them very tired. Changes in time zones and irregular hours of work also make this job difficult.

Sometimes the work is dangerous. Flying through rough weather makes planes bounce around. Dishes and glasses can fall. Passengers can get sick, and sometimes they even get hurt. But a well-trained steward or stewardess always manages to remain calm.

Even though *it doesn't say so* in the story, you can tell that:

a. This job is very easy.

b. Being a steward or stewardess is not glamorous and exciting all the time.

c. The job of a steward or stewardess is not dangerous.

d. Stewards and stewardesses must know how to fly a plane.

A Cure for
Those Who Miss Vocabulary

Finding meanings of words in paragraphs is easy—*if you know how.* You must be like a detective. You must learn to spot clues that tell you the meanings of words. Once you learn to spot clues, you can become a good "word detective." You will be able to find the meanings of words easily.

One kind of clue used most of the time to give word meanings is a *context clue.* This means that the way the word is used in the sentence tells you what it means.

Look at the example.

Example One:

Because the sun was hidden by thick, gray clouds, the day was *gloomy.*

What is the meaning of *gloomy*? The context clue (the way *gloomy* is used) tells you what it probably means. Since the sun was hidden by thick, gray clouds, the day was probably dark, not bright. This is the meaning of gloomy. *Gloomy* means dark, without light or brightness.

Try some other examples. Use context clues. Be a good word detective.

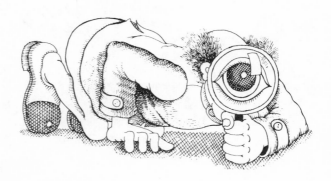

Use the context clues given to try to figure out what *slain* means. Look at the sentences carefully. Police gunfire was used against the robbers. This is your first clue. The second clue is that bodies lying in the street are usually dead people (especially when police have been shooting at them). Put the clues together to figure out the meaning of slain. The most logical answer (and the correct one) is that *slain* means killed.

The word *obese* means:
    a. tall. **b.** muscular. **c.** handsome. **d.** fat.

The best answer is *d.* All the context clues tell you the man is overweight. *Tall* might seem like a good answer because a tall man might not fit through a door. But the other clues show that *obese* means fat, or overweight.

Example Four

Not many people like Alice because she is so *vain*. She thinks she is the prettiest girl in the class. She also thinks she is the smartest. She even tells everyone that she thinks these things.

The word *vain* means:
    a. queen of the class.
    b. thinking you are better than others.
    c. smart.
    d. well-liked.

At first, *a*, *c*, and *d* might seem like good answers. But the context clues tell us Alice is not well-liked because she thinks she is better than the other students. Therefore *b* is the answer.

The police had the prisoner by the arm. As they got out of the car, the convict tried to *bolt.* He was fast. He got halfway down the street and tripped over a bicycle. The police were able to catch him and put handcuffs on him.

The word *bolt* means:
    a. shoot. **b.** fight with fists. **c.** run away.
    d. disappear.

The best answer is *c, run away.* The context clues tell us that the prisoner was fast. They also tell us he got halfway down the street before he tripped. These clues tell us he was trying to run away.

Sometimes you can tell what a new word means by the sentences that are near it. Often these other sentences give a definition of the word. Look at the examples.

Example One

The snake's head was *severed*. They found its body in one place and its head in another.

The word *severed* is new. What does it mean? If you read carefully, you find that it means "cut off." The snake's body was in one place and its head in another. Bodies and heads are not separate unless one of them is cut off.

Example Two

After working for 26 hours, the man went home to *slumber*. He slept for over 12 hours.

The word *slumber* means "sleep." The man was so tired from working he needed to slumber. He slept for over 12 hours.

If you are alert when reading, you will be able to figure out a lot of new words. Meanings are often given. But you have to know how to find them. If you are on your toes, you will become a great word detective.

A Final Word on Vocabulary

The key to improving your vocabulary is interest and a real desire to improve. Once you have this interest, you will find plenty of opportunities to learn new words. Coaches, teachers, fellow students, television announcers, books, newspapers, and magazines can all help you to find new words. But just hearing new words and doing nothing else is useless. *Effort* is the most important part. The following steps have helped many students learn hundreds of new words easily:

1. When you hear or read a new word, *write it down.* Ask what the word means or look it up.

2. Take some 3 x 5 index cards and cut them into little strips.

3. On one side of the strip write the word you want to learn. On the other side write a synonym (a word that means the same thing) or a short definition. The trick is to use a synonym or brief definition that you know and can remember. A long definition or a synonym that you don't know well will just make learning the new word more difficult.

4. Carry the cards with you as much as possible. Whenever you get a little time—waiting in lines, riding buses, before dinner, before bed, wherever you are—whip out your cards and practice. Look at the word you are trying to learn and try to think of the definition. When you do, turn the card over and check it out.

5. Practice until you master the word. Once again, *overlearning* is the secret to real mastery.

6. Use your new words as often as you can, even if you occasionally misuse a word. Before long, your new vocabulary words will become part of your everyday speech.